This is a coming of age story...
unfortunately for me
it's my parents who
are coming of age

A Newmarket Pictorial Moviebook

Newmarket Press • New York

IN AMERICA

a portrait of the film

Original Screenplay and Introductions by Jim Sheridan &
Naomi Sheridan & Kirsten Sheridan

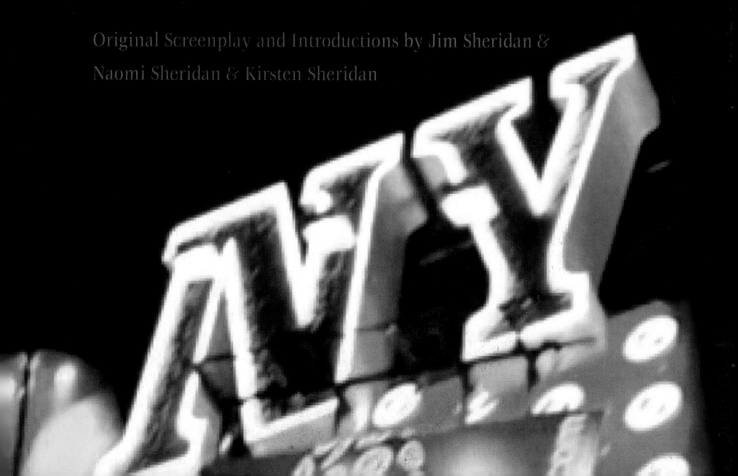

First Edition

10 9 8 7 6 5 4 3 2 1
1-55704-618-2 (Paperback)

Library of Congress Cataloging-in-Publication Data available upon request.

QUANTITY PURCHASES
Companies, professional groups, clubs, and other organizations may qualify for special terms when ordering quantities of this title. For information, write Special Sales Department, Newmarket Press, 18 East 48th Street, New York, NY 10017; call (212) 832-3575; fax (212) 832-3629; or e-mail mailbox@newmarketpress.com.

www.newmarketpress.com

Design Director: Deborah Daly
Editor: Healey Hubly Young
Creative Consultants: Stephanie Allen
J&A Advertising
Production Art Director: Kevin Corcoran
Photo Editor: Paula Davidson
Photographer: Barry Wetcher
Photographer: Bernard Walsh
Contributing Photographer: Brandy Eve Allen

MANUFACTURED IN THE UNITED STATES OF AMERICA

Other Newmarket Pictorial Moviebooks include:

The Alamo: The Illustrated Story of the Epic Film
Cold Mountain: The Journey From Book to Film
The Hulk: The Illustrated Screenplay
The Art of X2: The Collector's Edition
The Art of X2: The Making of the Blockbuster Film
Gods and Generals: The Illustrated Story of the Epic Civil War Film
Chicago: From Stage to Screen—The Movie and Illustrated Lyrics
Catch Me If You Can: The Film and the Filmmakers
Frida: Bringing Frida Kahlo's Life and Art to Film
E.T. The Extra-Terrestrial: From Concept to Classic
Windtalkers: The Making of the Film about the Navajo Code Talkers of World War II
Ali: The Movie and the Man
Planet of the Apes: Re-imagined by Tim Burton
Moulin Rouge: The Splendid Book That Charts the Journey of Baz Luhrmann's Motion Picture
The Art of The Matrix
Gladiator: The Making of the Ridley Scott Epic
Crouching Tiger, Hidden Dragon: A Portrait of the Ang Lee Film
The Age of Innocence: A Portrait of the Film Based on the Novel by Edith Wharton
Cradle Will Rock: The Movie and the Moment
The Sense and Sensibility Screenplay and Diaries
Saving Private Ryan: The Men, the Mission, the Movie
Bram Stoker's Dracula: The Film and the Legend

contents

Foreword by Jim Sheridan

When I get an idea for a film, I will run it through in my head and then compare it to the stories of James Joyce. For me, Joyce is like a litmus test. His stories are like an X-ray of Irish society viewed through the refined lens of the man who, after Shakespeare, knew more about world myth than any other writer. And he knew about myths the way a writer knows, not as something given and academic, but as something that could be changed like the dial on a radio. I often feel that Shakespeare was like a 2,000-year-old radio and he just adjusted the dial one tenth of an inch and received the old Greek plays with perfect reception and then he changed the myths ever so slightly to adjust to his own society.

When I decided to do *In the Name of the Father*, I thought about the fact that there were no good fathers in Irish literature. In Joyce, the only really good father is Leopold Bloom, the Jewish hero of *Ulysses*. I wrote Giuseppe Conlon's character in *In the Name of the Father* often with Bloom in mind.

When I was doing my own story, I thought a lot about Bloom and his dead son, and the resonance throughout *Ulysses*, of Shakespeare, and of *Hamlet* in particular. And when I wondered if it was right to do such a personal story and cannibalize my own life, I remembered that the great Shakespeare had a child called Hamnet and that three years after his son's death, he took out an old play and rewrote it.

And not only did he rewrite it, he went in the lonely isolation of backstage, he put on the armor of a dead man, and he clunked out on stage as the ghost of Hamlet's father. That idea has always struck me as profound. A live man in dead man's clothes talk-

Jim Sheridan with daughters Kirsten and Naomi in 1981

ing to his dead son, alive, in front of him, on stage and asking for revenge. Shakespeare must have been tough, I thought, to keep the deep baritone of the ghost intact. Bloom, too, ruminates on death incessantly because he lost his own son Rudy, who appears to him in the magic realism of the brothel in *Night Town*.

In literature it seems that a lot of writers have suffered the death of a sibling. The list includes Joyce, Wilde, Yeats, and Eugene O'Neill, and the painters Van Gogh, Dali, and I think Monet. I suppose I know these somewhat morbid facts because my brother Frankie died when he was ten and I was eighteen.

So when I thought about putting Frankie in *In America*, I realized I would be my own father and that my own daughter would be me (in the screenplay). And then I thought of Angelica Huston in her father's (John Huston) wonderful swan song, *The Dead*, and I thought about Molly Bloom withholding sex from Bloom because of the death of Rudy and I thought, Holy God, it's only a movie, I better have a happy ending.

And I decided that I would do a love triangle between Johnny and Sarah where they both have to let the dead loved one go. And then I had the picture: the thematic idea of the Irish leaving death behind and traveling to the new land where they were accepted. So I took out the pages again, and into the episodic tale that was my life, I entered as my own father. And in a sense I became born again.

J.S.
Dublin, September 11, 2003

Foreword by Naomi Sheridan

It was night, we were one of the few cars on the road and I, at nine years old, was starting to think, "Where the hell is this America place?" when we noticed the cop car behind us.

"Does he want us to stop, do you think?" my mam, who was driving, asked my dad.

Unperturbed, my dad looked in the rearview mirror. "No I don't think so," he said.

"Then why are his lights flashing?" my mam asked nervously.

My Dad came back briefly from whatever story-world he was inhabiting. "Sure, they always have them on, you're fine."

"I don't know," my mam said doubtfully. I have to say initially I shared my mam's doubt by then, but then I remembered in every film I'd seen they were indeed flashing their lights, so maybe my dad was right.

However, when, ten minutes later, the cop announced over the megaphone, "Lady, pull into the side of the road," there was no doubt left in our minds. As he approached our car, I wondered, did he think my mam was a criminal, as we had ignored his signals for the last ten minutes. I couldn't think of my mam as a criminal, knowing she wouldn't even eat a grape in the supermarket without paying for it.

"You were going over the speed limit," he said, glaring at us through his amber sunglasses. Afterward, my mam said she thought she was being arrested by Rod Steiger (his character from *In the Heat of the Night*).

"Eemmm," my mam said, "I'm from Ireland, and we go by kilometers instead of miles."

He waited for her to finish and, when he realized she already had, he said, "Lady, that's the worst excuse I've ever heard. Follow me." We followed him to the judge's house, who answered the door in his bathrobe. My mam and dad disappeared inside and I watched their silhouettes from outside.

My younger sister, Kirsten, who had been asleep through this whole ordeal, finally started stirring. I waited for her to wake with bated breath, ready to drop this bombshell. She looked up at me through squinted eyelids.

"Kirsten," I said with glee. "Mam and Dad got arrested!!"

Kirsten, still half asleep, looked at me crankily. "So what?" she uttered before going back to sleep again.

When my mam and dad finally came back out, my dad appeared to be the best of friends with "Rod Steiger." He was asking him for a loan of $6 for the toll, as he had literally given his last dollar away toward the fine. He was saying he would mail it back as soon as we got to New York. "Sure, sure," the cops laughed.

"No, seriously," my dad assured, "I will."

Thankfully, after that we were on our way, and soon after arrived in New York City. I remember our first impression of the city. We were overwhelmed by the lights, all the people and the vibrancy of the place itself. My dad got the job he had been promised and, to celebrate, he took us to a restaurant for dinner.

"Kids, yiz can order whatever yiz want," he announced grandly.

I looked over the menu. "I'll have the lobster," I said.

My dad looked bemusedly at my mam and rolled his eyes. She gave him one of her looks that said, "You're on your own, kiddo." My dad looked back at us.

"Yiz can have everything but the lobster," he said, shattering my illusions of grandeur.

They were an eventful couple of days and I think the way we felt over those two days came to represent the things we felt over the next few years—fear, excitement, happiness, apprehension, and who knows what else. I think that's why those times stayed so firmly entrenched in my dad's mind. Over the ten years after we left America he would still frequently mention it.

But I also think he wanted us to do the screenplay, 'cos it's not just our story.

Above: My sister Kirsten (right) and me on St. Patrick's Day, 1981

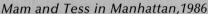
Mam and Tess in Manhattan, 1986

The last chapter in our story was the birth of my sister Tess who came into the world with a jolt. She was six weeks premature. My dad was acting in a play when my mother went into labor, and we had to go get him. He had his hair dyed steely gray for the role, and I remember wondering, would the doctors think the shock of Tess coming so early had sent him gray overnight?

Anyway, it was great after so much talk and speculation to see the finished product. And I can say the thing I was most thankful for was the brilliant cast. I thought they were all great, and the two girls, Sarah and Emma Bolger, seemed instinctively to know exactly how to play their roles perfectly.

That's it. I wouldn't take any of it back, and it was worth the experience. But, after writing this, one question sticks out in my mind more than anything else: Did Rod Steiger ever get his $6??

N.S.
September 9, 2003

Millions of people from all over the world have had their own experiences as immigrants in America. I remember we thought our apartment was small until we realized the Mexican couple upstairs lived in the same size apartment with their six kids! That made us think a little differently. And, like all the other people from different countries, we missed the country we had come from and our family and friends there. But, in a way, it made us closer. I don't want to paint a falsely rosy picture—I mean there were days when we wanted to kill each other—but I can definitely say my sister Kirsten was my best friend.

Foreword by Kirsten Sheridan

I was five when we went to America on a "holiday." Or at least that's what we had to pretend. To me it was home already because my family was there. And that was where home was.

My sister and I slept in a closet—a piece of wood magically turned into bunk beds (my mam was very resourceful). Naomi figured she'd get to Narnia quicker. Certain things I remember that I had never seen before—a bath in the kitchen, a cut-out half door (used for selling drugs) in the apartment on the first floor that we weren't allowed near, those roach motels, a police lock. To a kid these were all fantastic new props for my game of house.

My parents tried to make a game out of everything—when we had no chairs we suddenly became a Japanese family. Or, the best Christmas present ever: a letter from Santy explaining that he couldn't fit the computer in the sled.

I remember my dad always dancing and singing. A towel wrapped around him, dancing like an *eejit* to make you laugh. He never knew the words, but sang at the top of his voice. Walking down the street I used to look up at him. You could feel that he was the only person alive, always looking up at the clouds. And if you wanted to talk to him you had to go up there. Of course there were the hard times too—always being the new kid, your parents saying that you just had to be yourself (the worst advice ever!), feeling that embarrassment of having no money and thinking if you just had that Barbie bus you would surely fit in and start being the perfect family.

At those times I thought, this is a crap holiday.

I mostly remember my mam standing with her back to the wall, having come in from work with the bags of shopping (she never used to let me carry those bags—she said it balanced her to carry them all—I never believed her). My sister and I would run to her with shouts and accusations over whose fault something was. She would

Jim Sheridan and his future co-writer Kirsten Sheridan

lean back, the wall supporting her, feeling the weight of everything. Her eyes would close. And in that moment a silent make-up would dart between me and my sister.

My dad said being normal was boring. I tried to believe him. Then we saw *E.T.* We totally identified with him. My dad said *E.T.* wasn't about an alien, that it was about a little kid's search for family and identity. My sister and I thought he was mental.

We never did win that E.T. doll (as depicted in *In America*). But life is better than art—we got our own E.T. in the form of the little premature baby who craned her neck around to see us from the incubator.

In the form of Tess.

And we never did end up belonging to that perfect world. But who does? In the end, we always did belong in our family.

K.S.
September 8, 2003

12

the cast

sarah
samantha morton

johnny
paddy considine

christy
sarah bolger

ariel
emma bolger

mateo
djimon hounsou

13

the script

FADE IN

INT. JOHNNY'S CAR - DAY

Dark screen.

CHRISTY (V.O.)
There are some things you should
wish for...

Screen brightens to reveal an American flag
(soft focus) through passenger window.

CHRISTY (CONT'D)
...and some things you shouldn't.
That's what my little brother
Frankie told me. He told me I only
had three wishes. And I looked in
his eyes... and I don't know why I
believed him.

FADE OUT

EXT. IMMIGRATION - DAY

We are in a camcorder's point of view. It
zooms onto an American flag and then a sign
that says "US Customs."

We see two girls in the back seat of a car. The
older girl CHRISTY has a camcorder to her
eye. The younger girl ARIEL listens to her
father. All the family members have a thin
veil of perspiration over them from the hot
early summer.

Johnny turns, looks towards Christy and
Ariel.

JOHNNY
Remember, we're on holiday, all
right?

The mother Sarah shakes her head "no."

IMMIGRATION OFFICER
(through P.A.)
All those with U.S. passports, use
the two left lanes.

SARAH
Knock it off, Christy, love.

We see an Immigration Officer pass in front
of the car to the driver's side. Christy holds a
video camera – turns and aims it at the Immigration Officer.

IMMIGRATION OFFICER
(through PA)
All those with U.S. passports, use
the two left lanes.

SARAH
Christy.

She glances at Sarah, and then lowers the
video camera.

EXT. CHECKPOINT – DAY

Johnny's car sits amongst traffic.

The Immigration man's brow is wet from the
intense heat.

IMMIGRATION OFFICER
Passports, please.

Ariel volunteers information.

ARIEL
We're on holidays!

The Immigration man looks at her. He won-
ders, "Why did she day that?"

IMMIGRATION OFFICER
Are you, little girl?

Johnny hands the passports to the Immigration Officer.

ARIEL
Yeah, and my dad's not working.

The First Immigration Office immediately
gestures to a second Immigration Officer. The
second Immigration Officer approaches
Sarah's side of the car. Both officers look at
Ariel, who plays with a doll. Christy gently
pulls Ariel back as the Immigration men get
very formal.

1ST IMMIGRATION OFFICER
(to Johnny)

What's the purpose of your visit to the United States?

The Second Immigration Officer leans in to the open passenger window to question Sarah at the same time.

> 2ND IMMIGRATION OFFICER
> What are your purposes in visiting the United States?

> JOHNNY
> We're on holidays.

> 2ND IMMIGRATION OFFICER
> (to Sarah)
> And how long you been in Canada?

> SARAH
> Just visiting.

As Christy watches an officer come out of a booth with a dog, we hear her thoughts.

> CHRISTY (V.O.)
> Listening to my mam and dad...

> SARAH
> We got the car in Canada.

Christy sees the dog get up on top of the car and begin to sniff. A couple more Immigration men appear.

> CHRISTY (V.O.)
> ...I was scared we weren't gonna get across the border.

Sarah smiles as Second Immigration Officer leans against Johnny's car.

> CHRISTY (V.O.) (CONT'D)
> And if I didn't talk to Frankie...

> SARAH
> We were on holiday.

CHRISTY (V.O.)
...how were we going to get into America?

JOHNNY
Four weeks.

Johnny nods.

JOHNNY (CONT'D)
Well, she likes to... you know.

CHRISTY (V.O.)
"Please, Frankie...

CHRISTY (V.O.) (CONT'D)
...please...

The First Immigration Officer looks at the passports.

CHRISTY (V.O.) (CONT'D)
...please help us," I said.

Johnny turns and glances at Sarah.

1ST IMMIGRATION OFFICER
Er, how many children do you have?

JOHNNY
Er, three.

Sarah has heard this question in the middle of her own interrogation and answers as quickly as you can change focus.

SARAH
(to Johnny)
Two.

It focuses back lightning speed.

JOHNNY
Two.

1ST IMMIGRATION OFFICER
It says three here.

JOHNNY
Er, we lost one.

1ST IMMIGRATION OFFICER
(sighs)

The Immigration man looks at them, then at the passports. What he sees changes his attitude. He looks to his partner. They become protective.

1ST IMMIGRATION OFFICER
What's your name, little girl?

Ariel looks to her mother who nods for her to answer.

ARIEL
Ariel.

1ST IMMIGRATION OFFICER
And who are you?

Christy is stone cold silent. Ariel glances at Christy.

SARAH
She's Christy.

First Immigration Officer looks at Sarah, and then turns and looks at Christy.

1ST IMMIGRATION OFFICER
What age are you, Christy?

Christy will not answer.

>   ARIEL
>   She's ten.

First Immigration Officer smiles, then glances at Second Immigration Officer. He hands the passports to Johnny.

>   1ST IMMIGRATION OFFICER
>   Welcome to America.

>   JOHNNY
>   Thanks very much.

Johnny looks at Sarah, then glances at Ariel and Christy.

EXT. JOHNNY'S CAR – DAY

The family pulls away from the inspection post. Radio chatter is heard in the background.

>   CHRISTY (V.O.)
>   And that was my first wish used up.

The car passes into the background.

>   CHRISTY (V.O.) (CONT'D)
>   But I still have two left.

>   CUT TO:

EXT. HIGHWAY – NEW YORK – NIGHT

Pan with Johnny's car as it travels along the highway.

>   CHRISTY (V.O.)
>   We heard Manhattan before we ever
>   saw it.

Continue panning up and back to reveal Manhattan Island in the distance.

>   CHRISTY (V.O.) (CONT'D)
>   A thousand strange voices coming
>   from everywhere.

Traffic travels along the bridge.

>   CHRISTY (V.O.) (CONT'D)
>   And you're not going to believe
>   this...

F A C T :
Jim Sheridan, his wife Fran and their daughters Kirsten and Naomi moved to New York from Ireland in 1982 when the girls were five and nine years old respectively. After being arrested just miles into the U.S. from Canada, Sheridan was forced to spend the family's last $38 (and borrow $2 from the arresting officers) to buy their freedom.

INT. JOHNNY'S CAR – NIGHT

Johnny and Sarah in the front seat, backs to camera.

> CHRISTY (V.O.)
> ...but we had to go under the water to get to the city.

The car travels into a tunnel.

> MAN
> (to interviewer, through radio)
> No, I swear it. It was a real alien.

EXT./INT. JOHNNY'S CAR – NIGHT

Through rear window to Christy – Track with car as it travels. Christy stares forward.

> CHRISTY (V.O.)
> And we lost contact with everything. It was like we were on another planet.

She picks up a video camera, aims it forward.

On video camera screen held by Christy – we see Johnny throwing a Frisbee to Frankie. Track in.

Through windshield to Johnny. He looks forward.

Through passenger window to Ariel – she presses her face against the window.

> DJ
> (through radio)
> Classics from the '60s, '70s, '80s and '90s...

Through windshield to Johnny. He reacts, glances down at radio.

Down to Johnny's hand – he tunes the radio.

Through passenger window to Ariel. She turns and looks at Johnny.

> SONG
> (through radio)
> *It makes you feel happy*
> *Like an old-time movie*

Christy looks at Sarah and smiles.

> SONG
> *I'll tell you 'bout the magic*
> *And it'll free your soul*

Sarah looks at Johnny.

Johnny glances at Sarah.

> SONG
> *But it's like trying to tell a stranger*
> *'Bout rock and roll*
> *If you believe in magic*

Ariel sits up, leans forward, looking at signs.

EXT. STREET – NIGHT

The music on the radio continues.

> SONG
> *Don't bother to choose*
> *If it's jug band music...*

Along busy street (soft focus) – focus on a sign. It reads: "Radio City."

INT. JOHNNY'S CAR – NIGHT

Close up on Johnny as he drives the car.

SONG
...or rhythm and blues

EXT. JOHNNY'S CAR – CONTINUES

Pan and track in as the car turns and travels forward.

SONG
Just go and listen...

Track with the car as it travels along the busy street.

SONG
...it'll start with a smile
It won't wipe off your face
No matter how hard you try

Sarah leans through open passenger window. Ariel turns and looks at Sarah.

SONG
And we'll go dancing, baby
Then you'll see

On a video wall – The sign reads, "Times Square Gallery."

Through shop window to a television. The screen reads, "Come on in."

SONG
How the magic's in the music
And the music's in me

On busy street – Pan over the crowd.

Through windshield to Sarah – she turns and points.

Pan up to a video screen that shows an advertisement.

Through part-open passenger window – Christy clutches the video camera. She aims it in the foreground.

SONG
Do you believe in magic

Pan over building, pull back. An electronic

21

CINEMATOGRAPHY

When Cinematographer Declan Quinn was approached to shoot *In America,* he was intrigued. An acquaintance of Jim Sheridan's since the 80s, the two had many times discussed joining forces. The story sealed the deal for Quinn, who immediately identified with the Sullivan family and their struggle.

Following prep and principal photography, the shoot lasted about 10 weeks and took place in Ireland and New York. Quinn found working with Sheridan to be an eye-opening experience. "Part of the process is to try and get into his head," he says. "You need to get in there and stay there for the ride because Jim Sheridan is a very smart, intuitive person. The way he discovers things, the truth or the essence of a scene, is really fascinating. I try and stay with him and take it in and process that into a mood or a photographic kind of style."

Quinn found the crew to be equally admiring of the director and the free-flowing way in which he operates on set. "The electrics and the grips, the camera team, everyone really respects him because they appreciate that what he's doing is real cinema...they'll bend over backwards to make it work."

He continues, "A lot of people in cinema are kind of frozen in fear because of the producers, the schedule. Jim doesn't have so much fear. He just says, 'Well, it's not right, so we gotta get it right first.'"

One of the more challenging aspects of collaborating with Sheridan was his desire to be able to move scenes around later on without continuity problems. Quinn explains: "You have to keep it generic enough that if things change in the cut, it won't be jarring, but at the same time will maintain a mood that fits the emotion of the scene. It was a great challenge for me."

The New York scenes were shot "documentary-style" in and around downtown and the Tompkins Square Park area with a small crew, a few camera carts and some long lenses. "We wanted to use as much of the reality as we could," Quinn says.

In the end, Quinn was pleasantly surprised to see that nearly all of his shots made it to the final piece. "They may have been abbreviated, or a narrative or music was added, but in the end, it created this kind of montage to move the story along that was beautifully cut together."

billboard reads "Yes You Can."

On Johnny's car – Sarah taps her hand against the door.

> SONG
> *Yeah, believe in the magic*
> *Of a young girl's soul*

Sarah turns and looks at a woman – she gestures.

Through part-open passenger window to Ariel. She looks at the woman.

Pan and tilt down over signs.

> SONG
> *Believe in the magic of rock and roll*

On man (soft focus) – Pull focus as he looks forward.

On two young men. Pan as they walk.

Through windshield to Johnny. He smiles.

> SONG
> *Believe in the magic*
> *That can set you free*

Pan past buildings, then track along busy street. Tilt up to reveal a taxi traveling toward the foreground.

> SONG
> *Ohh, talking 'bout the magic*

Through part-open passenger window to Christy. She smiles.

> SONG
> *Do you believe in magic*

Continue panning.

> SONG
> *Like I believe in magic*

EXT. STREET/APARTMENT BUILDING – DAY

Pan up to an apartment building.

> SONG
> *Do you believe, Believer*

A bus passes in the foreground.

INT. MATEO'S APARTMENT – LIVING AREA – DAY

We see a formidable black man stare out his window, which is strangely decorated. We see his point of view of Heaven, which is in focus all on it's own. Then the focus changes to reality and the family car comes into the picture. The man screams.

> CHRISTY (V.O.)
> We looked all over Manhattan for a place to live. 'Til finally we found the house... of the man who screams.

The car pulls up to the building. Mateo looks down at Johnny's car.

Johnny opens the door, climbs out.

In Christy's camcorder the building looks like an ancient monument still clinging to faded elegance. As she pans down the building there is a flash of lightning from the strangely decorated window. She pans on down to the sudden smiling face of a Hispanic man called PAPO. He says into the camcorder.

> PAPO
> What are you doing with the camera, little girl?

Christy climbs from the car, clutching the video camera.

> PAPO (CONT'D)
> Are you the police?

> SARAH
> What?

> JOHNNY
> (to Ariel)
> Fingers.

Johnny closes the car door.

                              PAPO
                    Are you the police?

                              JOHNNY
                    No, we're Irish.

                              PAPO
                    All Irish are police.

                              SARAH
                    We're not.

Sarah takes keys from a bag.

                              ARIEL
                         (to Sarah and Johnny)
                    Are we going to live here now?

                              PAPO
                    You're gonna live in here, in this
                    building?

                              JOHNNY
                    Yeah.

Papo looks at the kids, a mixture of pity and
affection.

                              PAPO
                         (nods)
                    All right.

Papo holds out a cup as a man steps up to
them.

                              PAPO
                         (to the man)
                    Keep an eye on their car.

The man takes the cup.

                              PAPO
                         (to Johnny and his family)
                    Papo's gonna keep you safe now. All
                    right?

Papo opens the door for Sarah, Ariel, Johnny
and Christy.

                              PAPO (CONT'D)
                    Come on in. Welcome to your new
                    mansion.

Papo follows them inside. The man sits down.

INT. APARTMENT BUILDING – ENTRANCE HALL
– DAY

Pan as the door opens to Papo, gesturing to
Johnny and his family.

                              PAPO
                    Come on.

Christy, Ariel, Sarah and Johnny enter
through the doorway.

                              ARIEL
                    Look, a lift!

Ariel runs around Papo toward the elevator.

                              PAPO
                    That hasn't worked forever. Come
                    on, come on.

He gestures. Ariel looks up at him.

INT. APARTMENT BUILDING – STAIRS – DAY

Papo, Johnny and Sarah climb the stairs.
Behind them are Christy and Ariel.

                              ARIEL
                    Are we going to live here now?

                              CHRISTY
                    Yep.

                              ARIEL
                    Why?

They continue climbing the stairs.

                              CHRISTY
                    Nowhere else will take us.

                              ARIEL
                    Why?

                              CHRISTY
                    They don't want kids in Manhattan.

                              ARIEL
                    Why?

                              CHRISTY
                    Why do you think they call it Man-
                    hattan?

The stairs are completely dark except for a

shaft of light from the roof light that illuminates a door with the words "Keep Away" painted on it. A terrifying scream comes from the apartment followed by another flash of light.

            TONY (O.S.)
           (calls out)
     Papo.

Tony, clutching a bicycle, looks down at Papo.

            TONY
     Yo... Papo, don't come any further, man.

Tilt down off him to reveal a blind man. Papo enters and looks up.

            PAPO
     Yo, relax, Tony. It's just me.

Tony gestures with the bicycle wheel.

            TONY
     I know who the hell it is, man. Go back downstairs to your apartment.

Steve opens door, steps forward. Papo's girlfriend is seated in the background. She pulls on her top.

            PAPO (O.S.)
     I'm clean, man. I'm showing this family the empty apartment.

Tony stops, looks up. He pulls on a tee shirt.

            TONY (O.S.)
     No way, Papo.

            PAPO
     All right!

Christy enters.

            JOHNNY
     You're all right, Papo. I'll take over from here.

Johnny and his family move to climb the stairs.

SHOOTING IN NEW YORK

In America was one of the first productions to shoot in New York following the events of September 11, lending to the crew a strong sense of wanting to reveal the underlying soul of New York in the photography. To do this, Sheridan worked closely with award-winning cinematographer Declan Quinn.

"It was fantastic working with Declan," says Sheridan. "It was the first time I've ever worked with an Irish cinematographer and we felt very at home together. He also moved from Ireland to America when he was a kid, so he has his own very personal perspective on the story."

Quinn and Sheridan agreed that the look of the film should be intensely intimate, with the camera essentially becoming caught up in the emotional turmoil of Johnny and his family. At the same time, Quinn went for an almost dreamy, heated look that evokes the magic at the heart of the film. "One thing about Declan is that he has a brilliant sense of color," says Sheridan. "He gave the film a kind of Spanish magical realism quality that turned out to be exactly the right visual tone for a story of this weight."

Shooting in New York brought the story full circle for Sheridan, as he traveled the city he had once come to as a cash-strapped immigrant. He says: "I never could have set In America anywhere other than Manhattan...it's a tough city but it is fundamental to this story. This is a hopeful, loving story about New York."

MATEO (O.S.)
(scream)

Tony enters clutching the bicycle. Sarah and Ariel enter, climb the stairs, followed by Johnny and Christy.

ARIEL
(to Christy)
Why does he scream?

CHRISTY
Maybe he sees ghosts.

They continue on as Tony exits.

ARIEL
(to Christy)
Is this a haunted house?

INT. APARTMENT – LIVING AREA/STAIRWELL – DAY

Close on the key as it turns in the lock. With the family on the other side of the door we can see the typical Manhattan dead bolt stick that slides across as Sarah opens it from the other side. Then another huge lock opens.

INT. APARTMENT – HALLWAY - CONTINUOUS

Ariel swings from the banister.

SARAH
It's like Fort Knox.

ARIEL
Cool.

CHRISTY
(to Ariel)
Where did you learn that?

Sarah unlocks the door.

ARIEL (O.S.)
What?

CHRISTY
(shaking her head "no")
Cool.

ARIEL (O.S.)
I just heard it.

Sarah opens the door.

CHRISTY
You're American already. It's disgusting.

They walk through the doorway.

ARIEL (O.S.)
Race you in Christy.

SARAH (O.S.)
Oh, it's huge!

INT. APARTMENT – LIVING AREA – CONTINUOUS

Sarah and Johnny enter the apartment. Christy and Ariel hurry across the room.

ARIEL
I know, it's enormous.

CHRISTY
This is my room.

SARAH (O.S.)
It's big, girls.

Christy and Ariel continue through the door.

ARIEL (O.S.)
This is my room.

CHRISTY (O.S.)
I get top bunk.

Christy and Ariel step through the doorway.

CHRISTY
I get top bunk.

ARIEL
Look dad, there's a bath in the middle of the room.

Christy and Ariel run around the bath. Sarah runs to Johnny, they embrace. Christy opens the shutters on a window. The light from the

"Samantha Morton is like emotional quicksilver with an ability to go to amazing depths but also to stay grounded. I think she's one of the best performers of her generation, and that's why I picked her for Sarah."
—Jim Sheridan

"The film is ultimately
about wonder.
It's about trying to see the world
with a kind of child-like,
magical quality.
It's a view of Manhattan
as an island of dreams
that helps a family rediscover
their deep bonds.
I also like to think of it as
a love poem
to my wife and kids."
—Jim Sheridan

window floods into the room and illuminates about ten pigeons that fly around. Christy turns as pigeons scatter.

                    CHRISTY
          Wow, there's pigeons!
          Ariel, come look at this.

Johnny embraces Sarah.

                    JOHNNY
              (to Sarah, softly)
          It's a bit of a hole.

He looks at Christy and winks.

                    SARAH
          It'll be fine when we do it up.

                    JOHNNY
          It'll cost us, Sarah.

Sarah climbs onto a ladder.

                    JOHNNY
          How are we gonna pay for this
          place?

                    SARAH
              (leaning against him)
          We'll sell the car.

                    ARIEL (O.S.)
              (to pigeons)
          Whoosh, whoosh! Come on!
          Whoosh, whoosh!

                    JOHNNY
              (glancing around)
          Are you okay?

                    SARAH
          Mmm. Yeah, good.

She leans back, looks down.

                    JOHNNY
          Are you?

                    SARAH
          I'm great.

                    JOHNNY
          Are you?

She looks at him.

                    ARIEL
              (to pigeons)
          Whoosh, whoosh...

                    ARIEL (O.S.)
          Dad?

                    JOHNNY
          What?

                    ARIEL (O.S.)
          Can we keep the pigeons?

Ariel hurries forward.

                    ARIEL
          Dad, can we keep the pigeons?

                    ARIEL (CONT'D)
          Hello... Dad?

Johnny turns and looks down at Ariel.

                    ARIEL (O.S.) (CONT'D)
          Can we keep the pigeons?

                    JOHNNY
              (nodding his head "no")
          No, we have, we have to leave them
          go.

Christy aims the video camera up at the pigeons. A pigeon flies off and lands on the skylight.

EXT. APARTMENT BUILDING – ROOF – DAY

On the skylight as the pigeons fly through it.

                    CHRISTY (V.O.)
          It seemed like all our problems were
          flying away.

EXT. STREET – DAY

Pan past Ariel clutching a wicker fan, to Christy clutching the video camera. Johnny and Sarah are clutching a sofa.

KALEIDOSCOPE

The production shot for ten weeks in Ireland, mostly interiors, but also some exteriors, including the scenes at the festival where Johnny loses the family's rent money in his quest to win a doll. "We realized it would have been hard to get the kind of flexibility we needed to shoot this film in a building in New York," says Arthur Lappin, "so we had production designer Mark Geraghty use his talent to re-create New York in Dublin."

Geraghty started with a massive old house—which Jim Sheridan calls "the Irish Taj Mahal"—and transformed its longs corridors and echoing rooms into a typical ghetto tenement, replete with the grit, grime and kinetic energy of New York. Not surprisingly, the set was rife with rumors that the house was haunted, but if so, the ghosts must have received quite a shock from watching their surroundings transform from an Irish sea-side mansion to a Hell's Kitchen hovel.

Says Jim Sheridan of Geraghty's sets, which were based in part on Sheridan's remembrances of furnishing and maintaining his family's home on pocket change and street-smarts: "I think places are a state of mind—Dublin can be New York because it's all in your mind—and Mark's set succeeded in bringing that place in my head fully to life."

After shooting in Ireland, the production headed to Manhattan to capture the ineffable rhythm and hue of New York's lower-class neighborhoods, shooting on the Lower East Side and Spanish Harlem and grabbing the pivotal footage of Manhattan buried under fresh snow. The emphasis here was on reflecting New York as a kaleidoscope of different cultures and attitudes.

"We weren't looking for the New York of famous buildings and landmarks," notes Lappin. "This film is more about what's going on in the streets, in the lives of ordinary people making their way in the city, and we were looking for the chaos and grit, as well as the underlying sense of community."

INT. SARAH/JOHNNY'S APARTMENT – LIVING AREA - DAY

Pan past Christy, seated on the floor, to Ariel and Johnny. Sarah is painting a pillar as Johnny paints a wall.

> ARIEL
> Dad, can I help?

> JOHNNY
> (turning)
> Go and ask your ma.

Ariel walks over to Sarah.

> ARIEL
> Mam, can I help?

> SARAH
> Why don't you go on your skates?

> CHRISTY (V.O.)
> I'll fast forward through this bit.

Speeded up, Sarah and Johnny paint as Christy stands, hurries out, followed by Ariel.

MATCH DISSOLVE – SPEEDED UP

Later – Sarah is standing on a stepladder. She paints a pillar as Ariel and Christy rollerskate. In the background Johnny paints a shutter.

MATCH DISSOLVE – SPEEDED UP

Later – Sarah is seated on a chair, Johnny is lying on a chaise lounge. Christy and Ariel rollerskate around them.

Sarah turns toward Christy and smiles.

INT. BAKERY – DAY

Close up on Ariel as she jumps up and down.

> CHRISTY (V.O.)
> Ariel got to know everybody in the neighborhood.

Ariel turns and looks toward the camera.

EXT. STREET – DAY

Pan across a busy street, down to a man pushing a bicycle. He waves.

INT. DRY CLEANERS – DAY

Close up on Ariel. A woman hands sweets to her.

INT. DELICATESSEN – NIGHT

A man clutches a paper bag. He looks to the camera and smiles.

EXT. STREET/ICE CREAM PARLOR – NIGHT

Through the window we see Sarah cleaning a table.

> CHRISTY (V.O.)
> My mam couldn't get a job teaching. So she got a job in the ice cream parlor...

EXT. STREET – DAY

Johnny walks along a busy street. He glances around.

> CHRISTY (V.O.)
> ...so Dad could go to auditions.

He continues forward – looks up.

INT. THEATRE – AUDITORIUM – DAY

Johnny shields his eyes from a spotlight.

> JOHNNY
> (to theatre director, without his Irish accent)
> I really like the character. I'm, I'm glad you asked me back. And I just wanna say I'm real pleased about that.

On Theatre Director, seated. A woman and the Assistant Director are seated behind him.

> THEATRE DIRECTOR
> (to Assistant Director)
> How about the part of Vinny? Has he looked at that?

JOHNNY (O.S.)
(without Irish accent)
The New York guy? He's a bit of a
stereotype, but if you want him, you
got him.

THEATRE DIRECTOR
Can you do a London accent?

JOHNNY
(with English accent)
What? You're having a laugh. He's
only got two lines. Do you want me
to come up there and sort you out?!
(he gestures)

The Assistant Director glances at the Theatre
Director.

ASSISTANT DIRECTOR
(to Theatre Director)
You like him?

THEATRE DIRECTOR
Yeah — but acting's about more than
just accents.

> "Jim has a very organic
> style. He's not the type of director
> who has everything all mapped out pre-
> cisely. Rather, he goes for a kind of
> honesty and truthfulness in each and
> every scene—and of course because
> he's also the writer, he can deviate from
> the script at any time. So, what I try to
> do is build a structure around Jim that
> gives him maximum flexibility and
> freedom to let that magic happen as
> much as possible."
> —Arthur Lappin,
> longtime partner and producer

> "I'm always trying to capture that invisible thing, the thing that's in front of your face that you can't actually see in the moment, but is very powerful. I'm looking for the authentic, but it's hard to say exactly how you get to that. It's not something you can 'direct' in the common sense of the word. You just have to keep the actors feeling like they're in charge of their lives and let it happen."
>
> —Jim Sheridan

INT. THEATRE – AUDITORIUM – LATER

The Theatre Director gestures as Johnny walks in.

> THEATRE DIRECTOR
> (to Johnny)
> I wanted to cast you, but you've got to give me more. Much, much more. Don't you understand?

> JOHNNY
> (nodding)
> Mmm-hmm.

> THEATRE DIRECTOR
> (gesturing)
> Get it out of your head. It's from here and from here.

> JOHNNY
> Just give me one more chance.

He looks long at the Theatre Director.

EXT. STREET – DAY

Pan up to apartment building.

> CHRISTY (V.O.)
> But he didn't get another chance.

Tilt and track in over the buildings.

> CHRISTY (V.O.) (CONT'D)
> And then summer came. And with it
> the heat.

Continue panning to reveal water towers.

> CHRISTY (V.O.) (CONT'D)
> And a new word — humidity.

Hold on the water towers.

INT. SARAH/JOHNNY'S APARTMENT – LIVING
AREA – DAY

Pan past Johnny's hands to Christy's reflection in a mirror. She looks up at an off-stage showerhead, as he turns the tap.

> CHRISTY
> Dad, it's still not working.

> JOHNNY
> Wait.

He leans against the wash basin.

> JOHNNY (CONT'D)
> Wait.

He wipes his brow.

Christy, standing in the bath, wears a swimming costume. Ariel is behind her.

And then summer came. And with it the heat.

And a new word — humidity.

> ARIEL
> It's too hot.

Christy turns and looks at the showerhead. Johnny turns the tap. She gestures.

> CHRISTY
> It's still not coming through the holes, Dad.

> JOHNNY
> Hang on there.

He gestures, steps forward.

> JOHNNY (CONT'D)
> Wait. Wait. It's coming — It's coming.

Christy looks at the showerhead. She reacts as water drips from it. She turns and looks at Ariel behind her.

> CHRISTY
> (to Ariel)
> It's working.

Christy and Ariel stand beneath the shower. Johnny steps toward them and embraces them.

> CHRISTY
> Well done, Dad. It's lovely and cold.

Johnny kisses her cheek. They embrace again.

> JOHNNY
> I love you. Jesus!

He shakes his head beneath the shower.

INT. SARAH/JOHNNY'S APARTMENT – LIVING AREA – LATER

Pan up to the showerhead – water pours from it.

> CHRISTY (O.S.)
> Sshh, Ariel. Dad has an audition.

Ariel and Christy are seated in the bath, behind a shower curtain. Johnny, seated nearby, clutches a script.

ARIEL
Dad?

JOHNNY
What?

The shower curtain opens, revealing Christy.

ARIEL
What are you doing?

JOHNNY
I'm reading a script.

ARIEL
Why?

JOHNNY
'Cuz I'm learning my lines.

Ariel closes the shower curtain, then opens it.

ARIEL
Dad, can we stay here all day?

JOHNNY
Mmm-hmm.

ARIEL
Dad, America's okay.

JOHNNY
Great.

Christy whispers to Ariel.

ARIEL
Dad?

JOHNNY
What?

He turns and looks at them.

ARIEL
Nothing.

Hold on Johnny as Ariel and Christy close the shower curtain.

INT. APARTMENT BUILDING – STAIRS – DAY

Sarah climbs the stairs. She stops and leans against the banister. She turns and sits.

INT. SARAH/JOHNNY'S APARTMENT –BATHROOM

JOHNNY
(with American accent)
What are we doing here? Huh? What are we doing here?
(he turns)
What are we doing here?
(he hits his head with the script)
What are we doing here?
(he turns and gestures)
What are we doing here, huh?

He leans into a mirror.

JOHNNY (CONT'D)
(with American accent)
What are we doing here?
(grabbing the mirror – shouts)
What are we doing here?!

CHRISTY (O.S.)
Dad, dad, Ariel's upset.

Pan to reveal Christy.

CHRISTY
She spent too long in the bath.

INT. SARAH/JOHNNY'S APARTMENT –LIVING AREA – DAY

Johnny passes Ariel, a towel wrapped around her.

JOHNNY
What's wrong with you?

He picks her up.

ARIEL
Our feet are like prunes.

JOHNNY
What?

ARIEL
They're like prunes!

He embraces her.

"When I read the script I understood Johnny right away... the way in which Johnny has lost faith was something I could identify with. I knew him. The film came to me at a time when I had lost faith in what I was doing as an actor. I felt that what I was doing was pointless and that was what really drew me to Johnny...and playing him has, in a way, really helped to restore faith in myself. Because that's what the film is about: it's about how you pick yourself up off the floor, get back on track and start believing again."
—Paddy Considine

JOHNNY
Oh Jesus, where's your ma?

He glances around.

INT. APARTMENT BUILDING – STAIRS – DAY

The door opens to reveal Johnny. He walks forward, stops to look down at Sarah.

JOHNNY
Are you okay?

Sarah, seated on the stairs, turns and looks up at Johnny.

SARAH (O.S.)
It's too hot.

He walks through the doorway and exits.

EXT. STREET – DAY

Johnny enters, pulling an air conditioner on a trolley.

CHRISTY (O.S.)
Dad, how are you gonna get that air conditioner up and down the path?

JOHNNY
Come on.

Christy follows him.

CHRISTY
Dad, how are you gonna...?

He tries to pull the trolley onto the sidewalk.

JOHNNY
Jesus! Come on. Come on you...

He kicks the air conditioner, then pulls the trolley around the curb.

JOHNNY (CONT'D)
Come on!

CHRISTY
Dad, they're gonna shoot ya!

Johnny pulls the air conditioner forward – traffic is seen in the background.

TRAFFIC DRIVER
(speaks in foreign language to Johnny)

Cars swerve around Johnny as he moves the air conditioner.

CHRISTY (O.S.)
Dad, look out!

DRIVER
(to Johnny)
Asshole!

A man comes into view – Johnny glances at him.

EXT. APARTMENT BUILDING – DAY

Ariel is seated on the fire escape. She looks down at Johnny.

ARIEL
(calling out)
Mam!

She points – Sarah leans out the open window.

ARIEL (CONT'D)
Look, it's dad.

Johnny continues to pull on the air conditioner as the cars swerve around him. She points down to her father. We see Johnny from their point of view walking along the wide avenue against the traffic, which is making a V around him. A car not seeing him bursts through and almost knocks him down.

INT. APARTMENT BUILDING – STAIRS – DAY

Steve looks at Papo, gestures.

STEVE
(to Papo)
You're using, Papo.

Papo gestures.

PAPO
(speaks to Steve in foreign language)

STEVE (O.S.)
You're using.

Papo turns to walk away.

STEVE (CONT'D)
No, no. Don't you walk...

Johnny bursts in the door and makes down the corridor being half dragged by the weight of the air conditioner.

Papo and Steve are in his way.

PAPO
(speaks to Steve in foreign language)

Papo turns and reacts as Johnny walks towards him. Papo jumps aside as Johnny flies past them to the bottom of the stairs.

PAPO
Oh.

Papo follows Johnny.

PAPO
(to Steve)
Hey, can I have some of whatever he's on?

STEVE
(to Johnny)
Crazy fucking Irishman.

A Mexican woman, seated, a child on her lap. Johnny enters from below, slowly carrying the air conditioner up the stairs. He leans it against the banister. The woman stands, fans him as Christy enters from below. Johnny clutches the trolley and continues climbing the stairs.

Johnny glances down at Christy and the Mexican woman.

JOHNNY
Christy, open the door.

CHRISTY (O.S.)
(calling out)

Mam, mam! Dad's got an air conditioner!

Johnny lifts the air conditioner and continues up the stairs.

CHRISTY (CONT'D)
He's coming! He's coming!

Christy runs forward as Sarah comes out of the apartment. Johnny is clutching the air conditioner.

JOHNNY
(to Sarah)
Go on, get away from me! Go on!

Sarah turns and hurries toward Johnny.

SARAH
Jesus, Johnny, you'll have a heart attack.

JOHNNY
Go on.

Sarah steps away – he continues forward.

JOHNNY (CONT'D)
Open the window.

CHRISTY (O.S.)
Open the window, mam!

INT. SARAH/JOHNNY'S APARTMENT –
HALLWAY – DAY

Johnny struggles with the air conditioner as
he walks through the doorway.

JOHNNY
(to Sarah)
Open the window!

Sarah turns and runs through the doorway.

CHRISTY
(calling out)
Mam, open the window.

ARIEL (O.S.)
(calling out)
Open the window.

Christy turns and steps through the doorway.

CHRISTY
(to Sarah)
Open the window.

INT. SARAH/JOHNNY'S APARTMENT – LIVING
AREA – DAY

Johnny hurries through the room. He stumbles as he places the air conditioner onto the
window ledge.

JOHNNY
(breathes heavily)

Sarah closes the window on it. Johnny leans
against the air conditioner, turns and looks at
Sarah. He kneels and lifts the air conditioner
plug. He becomes annoyed, throwing it to the
floor.

Johnny kicks the plug, turns and moves
toward the hallway. Ariel and Christy stand

on either side of the doorway, looking out
into the hallway.

ARIEL
(to Christy)
What's wrong?

Johnny leaves.

CHRISTY
(to Ariel)
Wrong plug.

INT. SHOP – DAY

Johnny counts money onto the counter. A
newspaper headline reads: "102 Degree! Sizzler."

Johnny looks down at the money, then at the
Shopkeeper.

JOHNNY
I'm twenty-five cents short.

SHOPKEEPER
(shaking his head "no")
That's no use to me. I gotta make a
living. Dollar ninety-nine.

JOHNNY
I'll give it to you tomorrow.

SHOPKEEPER
You're from the junkies' building,
right?

JOHNNY
So?

SHOPKEEPER
Look at that.

The Shopkeeper raises his hand to reveal a
scar across his palm.

SHOPKEEPER (CONT'D)
That's from holding the knife of a
junkie. I got twenty-five stitches, he
got probation.

JOHNNY
Do I look like a junky to you?

SHOPKEEPER
Dollar ninety-nine.

Johnny grabs the money. The shopkeeper watches as Johnny turns and leaves. He picks up a baseball bat.

INT. SARAH/JOHNNY'S APARTMENT –
KITCHEN/DINING AREA – DAY

Sarah picks up a bag of beer bottles. She turns, steps to the table, and takes the bottles from the bag, placing them in a box. Johnny comes back.

JOHNNY
(to Sarah)
What's that?

SARAH
There's five cents on each of those.

JOHNNY
(reacts)
Where's the hundred dollars I gave you?

SARAH
I put it in the bank like you insisted.

Johnny grabs the box, turns and walks into background.

Sarah glances at Ariel and smiles.

EXT. STREET – DAY

Johnny clutches the box of empty beer bottles as he strides across the street.

MAN (O.S.)
(to Johnny – shouts)
You're gonna get yourself killed!

Johnny glances at a car.

DRIVER
Hey, Superman, hurry up!

Johnny continues walking, exiting through a shop doorway.

INT. SHOP – DAY

The shopkeeper picks up the box of empty beer bottles. He places a coin onto the counter.

SHOPKEEPER
And twenty-five cents.

Johnny places money onto the counter. He looks at the shopkeeper.

JOHNNY
And two dollars. Mr. American Dream.

SHOPKEEPER
And one plug.

He places the plug on the counter. Johnny picks it up and exits. The shopkeeper holds up a coin.

SHOPKEEPER
And one cent.

Johnny re-enters, takes the coin from the Shopkeeper, and exits.

INT. SARAH/JOHNNY'S APARTMENT – LIVING AREA – DAY

Johnny fastens a screw to the plug with a knife.

Ariel steps up to him. Sarah fans herself with a hat.

ARIEL
Dad, don't worry, mam's breathing's okay.

He glances at Sarah.

JOHNNY (O.S.)
Is it okay?!

Sarah looks at Johnny and smiles.

ARIEL
(to Johnny)

It's the lemon drops, they're magic.
You take them... and you forget
about your breathing.

Sarah opens her mouth to reveal a sweet. She smiles. Johnny turns.

> JOHNNY
> (to his family)
> Say your prayers.

He plugs in the air conditioner.

> ARIEL
> Oh, wow.

> JOHNNY
> It's all right, Ariel.

Johnny lifts Ariel up.

> JOHNNY (CONT'D)
> Go on, get your head in there!

He swings Ariel up toward the air conditioner.

> JOHNNY (CONT'D)
> Is that good?

Christy stands and hurries forward.

> JOHNNY (O.S.) (CONT'D)
> Is that lovely? Yeah? Whoo-ooh!

> ARIEL
> Whoops!

> JOHNNY
> Get a load of that!

> ARIEL (O.S.)
> Get Christy!

Holding Ariel, Johnny places his arm around Christy's shoulder.

> JOHNNY
> (to Christy)
> Come on, get your face in there.
> Look at that.

They all lean in toward the air conditioner.

> CHRISTY/ARIEL
> (loud shriek)

Sarah fans herself with her hat. Christy nudges Johnny.

> CHRISTY
> You're a genius, dad.

INTERCUT/INT. APARTMENT BUILDING – BASEMENT – DAY

Close on a fuse box – a fuse blows up.

In the living room, everyone reacts as the air conditioner stops.

Close on the fuse box – sparks shower from it.

INT. APARTMENT BUILDING – STAIRS – DAY

Through the doorway we see Steve and residents of the building. They react as the lights go out.

> STEVE
> What's going on?
> (to Johnny)
> Hey, gringo!

Johnny glances around.

> STEVE (O.S.)
> (calls out to Johnny)
> Gringo, what the hell's going on up there?

EXT. STREET – DAY

A busy street leading to the apartment building.

> WOMAN (O.S.)
> (speaks to Johnny and his family in Spanish)

> CHRISTY (V.O.)
> We got out of there as fast as we could.

Sarah, Johnny, Ariel and Christy cross the street.

CHRISTY (V.O.) (CONT'D)
We went to the bank — took out our money... and went to the movies where it was lovely and cool.

A car turns.

INT. CINEMA AUDITORIUM – EVENING

An usherette glances around – Christy, Ariel, Sarah and Johnny are seated in the air-conditioned theater.

On screen – it reads: "ET: The Extra-Terrestrial"

EXT. STREET/ICE CREAM PARLOR – NIGHT

The ice cream parlor. A sign above it reads: "Heaven"

INT. ICE CREAM PARLOR – NIGHT

Marina, a waitress, looks down at seated Ariel.

MARINA
(to Ariel)
Listen, don't be upset. ET's gone to Heaven.

ARIEL (O.S.)
But they said he went home.

MARINA
Well, that's the same thing.

Ariel shakes her head "no."

ARIEL
No. It's not.
(to Sarah and Johnny)
I miss things.

She is afraid to say what it is.

Ariel looks at Christy. Johnny looks down at Ariel.

JOHNNY
What do you miss?

ARIEL
Things. I've no one to play with.

Johnny gestures to Christy. The parents know what she means.

JOHNNY
You have your sister to play with.

Ariel shakes her head "no."

ARIEL
No, she plays with her camcorder.

Christy glances at Sarah and Johnny.

ARIEL (O.S.) (CONT'D)
And I've no one to tell my secrets to.

Ariel looks at Johnny.

ARIEL (CONT'D)
Christy tells them to her camcorder.

She shakes her head "no."

ARIEL (CONT'D)
(whispers)
And she won't let me hear what she says.
(beat)
And you don't play with us any-more.

Sarah turns and looks at Johnny. Johnny looks down at Ariel.

JOHNNY
I do play with youse.

ARIEL
Not like you used to.

Johnny looks down. Everyone knows what she means. Sarah places her arm around Ariel's shoulders, kisses her head.

EXT. FAIR – NIGHT
A man on stilts walks in a crowd at a fair.

F A C T :
In the original script, Christy was the narrator but without the use of a camcorder. Ironically U2's Bono (who co-wrote the song *Time for Tears*) read the script and began to suggest that perhaps a camcorder would be a good way of depicting the drama, but Sheridan was a few minutes ahead of him...he had just returned from purchasing one to test out that very idea.

MAN
(to fairgoers)
Here you go.

1ST STALL-HOLDER (O.S.)
(to fairgoer)
Hey, come on over here, kid.

2ND STALL-HOLDER (O.S.)
(to fairgoers)
Come on, folks, step right up. Pop a
balloon to win a prize.

Christy, followed by Johnny, clutches the video
camera as she walks through the busy fair.

3RD STALL-HOLDER (O.S.)
(to fairgoers)
Pick a number. Pick a number.

ARIEL (O.S.)
(calls)
Dad, dad!

Ariel appears from the crowd.

ARIEL
Dad, you can win ET! You can win
ET!

She gestures, then turns and runs toward
background. Johnny enters with Sarah.

SARAH
Come here, come on.

EXT. STALL – NIGHT

Close-up on a bucket surrounded by ET dolls
– a ball bounces off the doll. We see a group
of teenagers at the stall throwing their balls.
The Barker collects two dollars from a kid
who has missed trying to win for his girlfriend. Another boy obviously has because of
the doll he holds.

BARKER (O.S.)
(to fairgoers)
It's a game of chance. It's as simple
as pie. It's a game of chance, as simple as pie.

Ariel, Christy, Sarah and Johnny approach
the stall. They stop.

ARIEL
(to Johnny)
All you have to do is throw the ball
through the hoop seven times and
you win ET.

JOHNNY
Seven times? Is that all?

ARIEL
(nods)
Yep.

Johnny looks at the Barker.

JOHNNY
(to Barker)
Can adults play?

BARKER (O.S.)
Sure.

SARAH
Be careful, Johnny.

ARIEL
Simple as pie.

Johnny glances at Sarah.

JOHNNY
Ah, sure, it's easy.

BARKER (O.S.)
(to a man)
That's two dollars.

The Barker counts banknotes as the man
throws a ball at the bucket.

BARKER
(to Johnny)
And you can keep throwing as long
as you double up your dollars. If
you win, you get every dollar back
and any prize you like.

Johnny toys with the balls.

DIRECTING

On his directing style, Sheridan says, "I am more for the humanist approach, which is that the people are very important. So, I'm trying to put the people center stage. And any camera move; you know those sweeping camera moves at rock concerts over the crowd to the singer? I just wish the camera would sort of go over and hit the singer out of the building, you know? That's the kind of shot I hate. Actually, a lot of shots I hate because they are full of mad ego and they're just demented.

"On the other hand, I wouldn't claim to know everything about camera work and stuff. I can fling the camera around on some kind of cranes, but I don't. I just think my visual world was based on the television set that didn't have vertical or horizontal hold. And the picture was capable of disappearing at any moment. So, although everybody else was secure in the fact that film is about pictures in front of your face, I am not. I think you can still have a film if there is no picture. And maybe that's mad, but it's what I come from. I think what you actually see on film is just an extension of what you feel, even if there is no picture. And sometimes the audience has to make their own film up to run concordant with the one they're seeing. So a lot of the times, the picture is actually in the darkness, between the frames, in the place where your mind escapes. There are not enough films where your mind can escape, and can play along with the film, and be engaged in a conversation about the presence. It's all cocaine kind of mad images, like from MTV."

JOHNNY
(to Barker)
You get all your money back if you
win?

BARKER (O.S.)
You get all your money back and
any doll you like.

He glances at Sarah.

JOHNNY
Oh, right.

BARKER (O.S.)
(to fairgoer)
That's two dollars.

The Barker tosses the ball out.

JOHNNY
(mumbles indistinctly)

We see Johnny start to throw.

SARAH (O.S.)
Whoops.

ARIEL
Yes!

Johnny looks at the bucket as his first throw
goes in.

JOHNNY
(softly)
That's one.

SARAH (O.S.)
Come on, Johnny.

Another successful throw.

JOHNNY
That's two.

He tosses a ball out.

The ball strikes the doll and misses.

BARKER (O.S.)
(to Johnny)
Two down, five to go. Four dollars.

ARIEL
Oh, damn!

Johnny counts out dollar bills.

JOHNNY
(to Ariel)
Come on, we'll get there, we'll get
there.

ARIEL (O.S.)
Come on, dad.

Close up on Christy.

ARIEL (CONT'D)
You're, you're excellent, you're brilliant.

JOHNNY
(to Ariel)
All right, don't worry. I'll get it in.

Ariel turns and looks at Sarah behind her.

ARIEL
Mam, is dad going to win?

SARAH
Of course he is, darling.

Sarah turns forward, jumps up and down.

ARIEL (O.S.)
Come on, dad.

Johnny throws the ball.

Close up on the bucket surrounded by dolls as
three balls fly into it.

MAN (O.S.)
All right!

ARIEL (O.S.)
Yes! Yes! Yes!

The Barker looks at Johnny.

BARKER
(to Johnny)
Three, four, five, very good. Only
two to go.

ARIEL
Yeah, whoo!

CHRISTY
Whoo!

Johnny looks at the bucket, then throws the ball. He reacts to the miss.

JOHNNY
(groans)

BARKER
(to Johnny)
Eight dollars.

Johnny places more bills onto the counter. The Barker gathers them up.

BARKER
(to fairgoers)
Game of chance, simple as pie.

JOHNNY (O.S.)
All right.

BARKER (O.S.)
(to fairgoers)
You can keep throwing as long as you double up your dollars.

Johnny throws the ball. It misses and bounces off the board.

ARIEL (O.S.)
Oh!

JOHNNY
Shit!

BARKER
(to Johnny)
Number five, two to go, sixteen dollars.

JOHNNY
Let's go for it.

Johnny picks up a ball – he leans back.

ARIEL (O.S.)
Come on, dad. Only two more to go.

Johnny tosses the ball into the air and catches it.

JOHNNY
(softly)
All right, it's all right, I'll get this. Don't worry.

He throws the ball, and misses.

JOHNNY (CONT'D)
(softly) Fuck.

He tosses the ball into the air and catches it.

BARKER (O.S.)
(to fairgoers)
Thirty-two dollars. We got thirty-two dollars over here.

JOHNNY (O.S.)
(to Barker)
I don't need a crowd.

The Barker turns and looks at Johnny.

BARKER
Well, you're the main attraction.

Johnny hands over the money. Sarah steps around him.

JOHNNY
All right, thirty-two, thirty-two. I'll get it, don't worry.

ARIEL
(whispers)
Come on, dad.

Johnny nudges Ariel.

JOHNNY
All right.

Johnny looks, then tosses the ball into the air. He catches it.

BARKER (O.S.)
(to fairgoers)
Game of chance, simple as pie.

As the crowd gathers, Johnny throws in

anger, and the ball goes in.

> BARKER (O.S.)
> (to Johnny)
> Oh, one to go one to go. One more throw for you. One more for the big doll for the little girl!

He throws the ball out.

> BARKER (CONT'D)
> (sighs)

The Barker steps forward toward Johnny.

> BARKER
> Sixty-four dollars. Are we finished, sir?

Johnny looks at the Barker. Sarah, behind him, searches through her bag as he takes money from his pocket.

> MAN (O.S.)
> Angela, over here.

> JOHNNY
> (to Sarah)
> I got fifty-five.

Christy takes money from her bag.

> SARAH (O.S.)
> Here, I have another five.

> JOHNNY
> Just need four more.

Christy holds out the money.

> ARIEL
> Dad, it doesn't matter.

Sarah takes the money from Christy.

> JOHNNY
> (to Sarah)
> Ah, no.

> SARAH
> (beat)
> Just take it, Johnny.

> BARKER (O.S.)
> (to Christy)
> And one dollar change for the big girl.

The Barker hands a dollar to Christy.

> BARKER (O.S.) (CONT'D)
> (to fairgoers)
> Only one to go.

The Barker looks at the other fairgoers.

> BARKER
> One ball to go over here. One ball to go for the big doll for the little girl.

He looks down at Ariel and smiles.

> SARAH
> Don't let him break your concentration, Johnny, yeah?

She pats his arm – he throws the ball.

The ball bounces off the edge of the bucket.

Christy looks at Johnny. Johnny glances down at Ariel and smiles. Then he turns and looks at Sarah.

> JOHNNY
> (to Sarah)
> Give me the rent money.

Sarah turns and looks at him.

> SARAH
> What?

> JOHNNY
> Give me the rent money.

> SARAH
> Oh, Johnny, please don't do this to me tonight.

> JOHNNY
> I can't lose in front of the kids again, Sarah.

Sarah removes a money-filled envelope from her bag. She places it on the counter, looks up

F A C T :
Jim Sheridan
truly did
bet all of his
money on a
carnival game
to win an E.T. doll
for Kirsten, but,
in real life, he lost.

at the Barker. She glances at Johnny.

STALLHOLDER (O.S.)
Three balls for a dollar.

Johnny counts out the bills.

BARKER
(to fairgoers)
Wait a minute, wait a minute, we
got a hundred and twenty-eight dollars over here.

Johnny picks up the ball and tosses it in the
air. He catches it and throws it. It misses and
bounces over the counter.

ARIEL
Oh.

1ST FAIRGOER
Oh, man!

2ND FAIRGOER
You can't ask him to do it again.

The Barker steps forward, gestures.

BARKER
We're finished now — sir.

The Barker moves to pick up the pile of bills.

SARAH
Leave it, please.

She takes more bills from the envelope,
places them onto the pile.

FAIRGOER (O.S.)
Wow, go for it, man!

The Barker looks at Sarah. She smiles.

JOHNNY
(to Sarah)
We can't blow all our money.

She glances at him.

SARAH
I believe in you and the kids believe
in you, and you can win that doll.
Go on.

ARIEL
Dad, you're gonna win, I just know
it.

CHRISTY (O.S.)
(softly)
Come on, dad.

Johnny tosses the ball into the air and catches
it. He looks over at Christy and Ariel. They
both place their hands over their eyes.

FAIRGOER (O.S.)
I'm too scared to watch him.

A couple stands on a balcony, watching
Johnny.

Christy looks at Johnny.

CHRISTY (V.O.)
And then I used all my willpower to
quiet the crowd.

SLO-MO

Johnny throws the ball – it bounces off a doll.

CHRISTY (V.O.)
But it didn't work.

SLO-MO

Johnny takes more bills from the envelope,
places them onto the pile. He picks up a ball.

SLO-MO

Johnny tosses the ball into the air and catches
it.

CHRISTY (V.O.)
Every cent of every penny we
owned was down for an ET doll
worth thirty dollars.

SLO-MO

Christy looks at Johnny.

CHRISTY (V.O.)
So I said... "Frankie — I have to ask
you for a second wish."

SLO-MO

Johnny looks down at Ariel – he throws the ball. The ball flies into the bucket.

CHRISTY (V.O.)
And to this day my dad still believes it was him who won the ET doll.

FAIRGOERS
(cheer)

SLO-MO

Johnny reacts, then looks down.

SLO-MO

Christy looks up.

CHRISTY
(mouths)
Thank you. Thank God.

SLO-MO

The Barker, shoulders down, picks up the ET doll. He turns and hands the doll to Ariel.

ARIEL
Oh my God! Yes!

Fairgoers jumping up and down, revealing a brass band performing.

EXT. FAIR – NIGHT

Johnny walks, followed by Sarah. He tries to grab Ariel.

JOHNNY
(growls)

STALLHOLDER (O.S.)
(to fairgoers)
Pick a number, pick a number.

JOHNNY
(shouts to Ariel and Christy)
Fee, fi, fo, fum...

INT. APARTMENT BUILDING – STAIRS – NIGHT

Outside Mateo's door.

JOHNNY (O.S.)
(shouts to Ariel and Christy)
I smell the blood of an Irish woman!

The door opens, revealing Mateo. He looks at Johnny.

Johnny, clutching Christy, Ariel behind him, hurriedly leaves.

JOHNNY
(to Christy)

Give me a bite of you, give me a bite of you!

He looks at Mateo.

Through the doorway, Mateo stares at Johnny.

> ARIEL (O.S.)
> Come on, Christy, come on.

> CHRISTY (O.S.)
> Run!

Mateo closes the door.

> ARIEL (O.S.)
> Run, ET!

Sarah places a blindfold over Johnny's eyes. Ariel clutches the keys, running.

> CHRISTY (O.S.)
> (screams)

> ARIEL
> Help!

> CHRISTY
> Ariel!

Johnny walks, beating his chest. Sarah is behind him.

> JOHNNY
> (shouts to Ariel and Christy)
> Fee, fi, fo, fum...

INT. MATEO'S APARTMENT – HALLWAY – NIGHT

On Mateo, listening.

> JOHNNY (O.S.)
> (shouts to Ariel and Christy)
> I smell the blood of an Irish woman!

On the stairs, Ariel tries to unlock the door.

> ARIEL
> Christy!

Christy runs forward.

> CHRISTY
> Ariel!

"Frankie —
I have to ask you
for a second wish."

ARIEL (O.S.)
(to Christy)
I can't reach the top lock.

She stops, turns and looks at Johnny.

JOHNNY (O.S.)
(shouts to Ariel and Christy)
Fee, fi, fo, fum...

CHRISTY/ARIEL
(scream)

JOHNNY
(shouts)
I... smell the blood...

INT. SARAH/JOHNNY'S APARTMENT – LIVING
AREA – NIGHT

Christy and Ariel enter the room, chased by
Johnny. He stops in the doorway.

ARIEL (O.S.)
(to the doll)
Run, ET. Run, ET, it's the monster.

JOHNNY
(to Ariel and Christy)
Fee...

Ariel climbs onto a chair – Christy hides
behind it.

ARIEL
(screams)

JOHNNY (O.S.)
(shouts)
...fi – fo...

Johnny steps forward.

CHRISTY/ARIEL
(screams)

JOHNNY
(shouts)
...fum...

Johnny continues forward – he moves his
arms from side to side.

JOHNNY (CONT'D)
(shouts)
...I smell the blood of an Irish man!

Johnny turns and drops to the floor. He
removes his blindfold. Sarah walks through
the doorway, walks towards him.

Christy crouches behind the chair. Ariel leans
from behind a pillar. She looks at Johnny.
Sarah is behind him.

SARAH
(softly)
Johnny, what's wrong?

JOHNNY
I was looking for him.

Johnny continues heartbroken. Christy
glances down.

JOHNNY (O.S.)
I was looking for Frankie.

Sarah leans into him. Sarah refuses to show
any emotion. She is aware that the kids could
be watching.

SARAH
(whispers)
Just play with the kids, Johnny.

He looks down.

JOHNNY
(whispers)
I couldn't find him.

Past the pillar to Ariel, who turns and looks
down.

JOHNNY (O.S.)
Am I going insane?

Sarah takes control. She gets right into his face.

SARAH
(whispers)
Just act, Johnny, just act. Go on,
love.

He looks at Ariel and Christy.

JOHNNY
(sighs, then growls)
Fee, fi, fo, fum...

When Johnny now plays the monster, it is with a scary intensity.

ARIEL/CHRISTY (O.S.)
(giggle)

JOHNNY
(inhales)
...I still smell the blood...

Ariel jumps from the pillar as he turns.

JOHNNY
(shouts, to Ariel)
...of an Irish woman!

Sarah turns and looks at Johnny. She smiles.

JOHNNY (O.S.)
(to Ariel)
Come on, give me your finger there!
Come on, give me your finger.

Christy and Ariel run – Johnny follows. The girls know this game.

CHRISTY
(screams)

ARIEL
Christy, I'll save you!

Ariel moves to hit Johnny with the doll. Sarah smiles. We can see that she loves Johnny and loves the love they used to have.

CHRISTY (O.S.)
No, dad...

Johnny clutches Christy. As he carries her, followed by Ariel – she strikes him with the doll.

SARAH
Johnny?

Johnny clutching Christy — he pretends to bite her as Ariel hurries to him.

JOHNNY
(growls)

ARIEL (O.S.)
(shouts)
No, get off her now, dad!

SARAH
Johnny?

Johnny clutches Ariel.

ARIEL
(whispers)
Christy.

Johnny removes the blindfold. He looks at Sarah.

ARIEL (O.S.)
No, dad.

SARAH
(to Johnny)
You didn't find me.

ARIEL
(giggles)

JOHNNY
I wasn't looking for you.

SARAH
Exactly. You weren't looking for me.

The next is the first romantic thing Johnny says and it is said through and beyond the pain of death.

JOHNNY
There's nowhere you could hide I wouldn't find you.

Johnny pushes Ariel aside. He pulls on the blindfold.

JOHNNY (O.S.)
(to Sarah)
Fee, fi, fo, fum...

Sarah smiles.

SARAH
Girls.

JOHNNY (O.S.)
(to Sarah)
...I still smell the blood...

She stands, picks up her handbag.

JOHNNY
(to Sarah)
...of an Irish woman.

CHRISTY (O.S.)
Mam.

Sarah searches through her handbag.

JOHNNY (O.S.)
(to Sarah)
Fee, fi, fo, fum...

She turns and hands the handbag to Christy.

SARAH
(to Christy)
Take the bag. Take the money. Go
to Heaven.

Sarah ushers them toward the door.

SARAH
(to Christy)
Marina'll look after you.

She follows them through the doorway.

JOHNNY (O.S.)
(to Sarah)
...I smell the blood...

Sarah closes the door.

JOHNNY (CONT'D)
...of an Irish woman.

Sarah walks through the doorway. She stops and
closes the door, looks at Johnny and smiles.

INT. ICE CREAM PARLOR – NIGHT

Christy and Ariel open the door and walk in.

MARINA
Oh, hi, you two.

A waiter waves to them.

WAITER
How are you girls doing?

ARIEL
(to waiter)
Hi.

CHRISTY
(to Marina)
Hi.

MARINA
(to Christy)
You're a little later than usual.

ARIEL (O.S.)
(to Marina)
Hi.

Christy and Ariel step to the counter.

MARINA
(to Christy)
Where's your mam?

ARIEL
My mam is playing with dad on her
own.

Marina smiles, looking at Christy.

INT. SARAH/JOHNNY'S APARTMENT – LIVING
AREA – NIGHT

Johnny raises his arms.

JOHNNY
Fee, fi, fo, fum...

Sarah stands in the center of the room and
starts to take off her clothes. She removes her
tee shirt.

JOHNNY (CONT'D)
...I smell the blood of an Irish
woman.

Johnny walks, then lunges towards Sarah.

JOHNNY
(breathes deeply)

Johnny steps past her. He turns, walks to her.

She unfastens her bra.

> JOHNNY
> Fee.... fi — fo...

He continues closer.

> JOHNNY (CONT'D)
> ...fum...

We are behind her, as she stands totally naked under the light.

> JOHNNY (O.S.)
> ...I still smell the blood... of an Irish woman.

Johnny grabs her, stops and feels along her body.

> JOHNNY
> (growls)

> SARAH
> (shrieks)

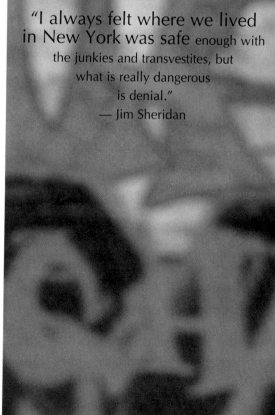

"I always felt where we lived in New York was safe enough with the junkies and transvestites, but what is really dangerous is denial."
— Jim Sheridan

He kisses her neck. His hands run along her shoulders and down to her breasts.

> SARAH (CONT'D)
> (chuckles)

> JOHNNY
> Where are the kids?

He moves to take off the blindfold – she places her hands against his face.

> SARAH
> Leave it on. Leave it on.

Sarah lowers her hands.

> SARAH (CONT'D)
> (whispers)

It's all right. It's okay.

She steps around him and moves to take off his tee shirt.

> JOHNNY
> Ah, where are the kids?

> SARAH
> They're fine. They're in Heaven.

She starts to take off his clothes.

> SARAH
> Marina's looking after them.

EXT. ICE CREAM PARLOR – NIGHT

Through the window we see Christy and Ariel

eating ice cream, watching as lightning flashes and rain starts to pour down.

EXT. APARTMENT BUILDING – NIGHT

Through the window we see Mateo in the shadows. He walks forward, stops. He leans against the window as lightning flashes.

INT. SARAH/JOHNNY'S APARTMENT – LIVING AREA – NIGHT

Sarah jumps onto Johnny's back.

> JOHNNY
> Come on to me.

Sarah reacts as he turns.

> JOHNNY (CONT'D)
> Come on.

> SARAH
> Oh, no!

He turns and grabs her as he spins around.

> SARAH
> No, no!

> JOHNNY
> Come on!

INT. MATEO'S APARTMENT – LIVING AREA – NIGHT

Mateo paces and seems agitated. He looks at one of his paintings. Suddenly he steps forward and slashes the painting with a knife.

INT. SARAH/JOHNNY'S APARTMENT – MAIN BEDROOM – NIGHT

Sarah sits astride Johnny as they fall onto the bed.

> SARAH
> (shrieks)

EXT. ICE CREAM PARLOR – NIGHT

Across the rain-soaked street and through the window, we see Christy and Ariel. Marina walks to them.

INT. MATEO'S APARTMENT – LIVING AREA – NIGHT

Mateo picks up a pot of paint and throws it. He then picks up a chair and throws it. He walks to a table and pushes paint pots off the top.

Across the darkened room, lights flash.

INTERCUT/INT. SARAH/JOHNNY'S APARTMENT – MAIN BEDROOM – NIGHT

Lightning flashes, revealing Sarah looking down at Johnny. Lightning flashes again, revealing Sarah in silhouette. Sarah and Johnny lying on the bed, as he pulls her to him.

> SARAH
> (shrieks)

Sarah lies on top of Johnny – they continue making love. They kiss passionately.

Mateo steps into the background. He pulls a painting to the floor, pulls over a rack.

Johnny kisses Sarah's neck.

Pan down to a canvas – blood drips onto it. Mateo's bloodstained hand enters frame.

> FADE IN

Johnny lies on top of Sarah as they make love.

> FADE OUT

Blood drips from Mateo's hand onto the canvas.

> FADE IN

Johnny lying on the bed, Sarah leans against him.

> CUT IN

Sarah lying on top of Johnny – she rolls toward him.

> CUT OUT

Sarah and Johnny lying in bed. They roll into the background.

> FADE OUT

Mateo leans over the canvas. He places his hand against it.

FADE IN

Sarah, back to camera, seated astride Johnny as they make love.

BLACK SCREEN

Mateo removes his hand from the canvas to reveal a bloody handprint.

DISSOLVE TO

Lightning flashes to reveal Sarah making love with Johnny.

EXT. NEW YORK – NIGHT

Pan across a darkened city – Lightning flashes in the background.

INT. SARAH/JOHNNY'S APARTMENT – BED-ROOM – NIGHT

           SARAH
           (breathes heavily)

Johnny looks at Sarah – she smiles, then she rolls away from him.

           JOHNNY
        What's wrong? Was it that bad?
           (beat)
        Look at me, Sarah.

Johnny sits up. He is bewildered. Sarah curls into herself.

           JOHNNY
        Are you all right?

He puts his hand on her back – shakes her. She is upset.

        JOHNNY (CONT'D)
        What's wrong?
           (beat)
        Come here to me.

He leans over her.

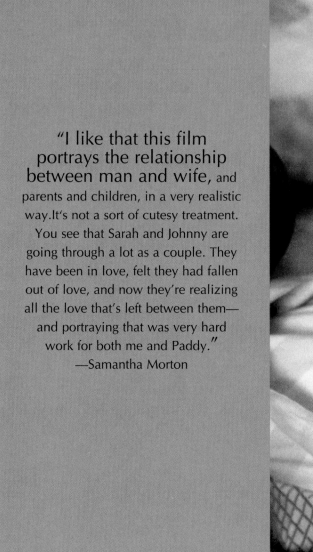

"I like that this film portrays the relationship between man and wife, and parents and children, in a very realistic way. It's not a sort of cutesy treatment. You see that Sarah and Johnny are going through a lot as a couple. They have been in love, felt they had fallen out of love, and now they're realizing all the love that's left between them— and portraying that was very hard work for both me and Paddy."
—Samantha Morton

           SARAH
           (softly)
        I can't.

           JOHNNY
        Come here to me.

He touches her shoulder.

        JOHNNY (CONT'D)
        Hey.

SARAH
(softly) I can't.

Sarah rolls over, clutches her hands over her face. It is clear Sarah is in tears.

SARAH
(sobs)

Sarah is a barnacle locked to the pillow. Johnny tries to turn her, she resists.

JOHNNY
(whispers)
Look at me and tell me the truth.

Johnny pulls Sarah's hands from her face.

JOHNNY (CONT'D)
(whispers) Come here.

She opens her eyes, and looks at him.

SARAH
Frankie had your eyes, Johnny.

Sarah tells him the truth. He lies back and stares up.

> SARAH (CONT'D)
> Say something.

Johnny continues staring up.

> SARAH (CONT'D)
> You blame me. I should have been there to catch him when he fell down the stairs. It's my fault.

> JOHNNY
> I don't blame you.

Johnny turns and rolls over. He closes his eyes, opens them and stares up.

INT. ICE CREAM PARLOR – NIGHT

Across the rain-soaked street, we see a group of transvestites running.

> 1ST TRANSVESTITE
> Oh, shit! Oh, shit!

They open the ice cream parlor door.

> 1ST TRANSVESTITE
> (to others)
> Hurry up.

A second transvestite moves aside as a man runs past him into the store.

> 2ND TRANSVESTITE
> Oh.

Ariel and Christy wave. Ariel looks at the second transvestite and waves.

> 2ND TRANSVESTITE (O.S.)
> (to Ariel)
> Hi, honey.

EXT. ICE CREAM PARLOR – NIGHT

Through the rain-soaked window we see Marina approach Christy and Ariel. She stops behind them.

EXT. PARK – DAY

Ariel walks along a path, kicking leaves.

> SONG
> *Oh, say can you see*
> *By the dawn's early light*

EXT. TAXI OFFICE – DAY

Johnny climbs into the driver's seat of a taxi.

> CHRISTY (V.O.)
> We had to go to a Catholic school, so my dad took a night job.

> EXT. PARK – DAY
> Ariel and Sarah rollerskate.

> CHRISTY (V.O.) (CONT'D)
> Ariel was worried about a blind man called Jose.

EXT. SCHOOL – DAY

> NUN
> (to school children)
> Everybody smile and say "cheese."

A photographer takes a shot of Ariel and the schoolchildren seated on steps, between nuns.

Naomi and Kirsten wearing their uniforms, 1982

SCHOOL CHILDREN
Cheese!

A flash flares.

Ariel and Christy walking along.

ARIEL
Christy, why can Jose not see?

CHRISTY
It's not Jose, it's...
(sings)
Oh, say can you see

INT. SARAH/JOHNNY'S APARTMENT – LIVING AREA – DAY

Christy picks up a plate and mug.

SONG
And the rocket's red glare

Johnny asleep in a chair. Ariel runs to him – she shakes him.

ARIEL
(softly)
Dad.

He wakes as Christy comes in, and places the mug and the plate on the table.

SONG
Gave proof through the night
That our flag was still there

ARIEL
(to Johnny)
I helped too.

He turns and looks at Ariel.

EXT. PARK – DAY

Ariel clutching a bag, Sarah clutching leaves in autumnal Central Park.

SARAH
Fill the bag with these, like that. Yellow ones.

ARIEL
Okay.

INT. ICE CREAM PARLOR – DAY

Sarah cuts silver foil from "wings" as Marina arranges feathers.

SONG
Oh say does that star-spangled
banner yet wave

INT. SARAH/JOHNNY'S APARTMENT – LIVING AREA – DAY

Christy is seated on the floor, between Ariel and Sarah. Ariel sticks leaves to a "costume" as Sarah picks up a leaf.

SARAH
(to Christy)
Maybe at the back like that.

She holds a leaf above Christy's head.

EXT. PARK – DAY

Ariel clutches a cup on a stick. Christy approaches, looks at the video camera screen.

ARIEL
Statue of Liberty... nation, friends... and caring... so now we're all together.

Christy walks forward – Ariel bows.

ARIEL
(to Christy)
I'm hungry!

EXT. STREET/THEATRE – DAY

Christy, Ariel and Johnny lean against a taxi. Christy puts money into a parking meter.

JOHNNY
(to Christy)
Right, keep your eye on the meter.

CHRISTY
Yeah.

JOHNNY
(to Christy and Ariel)
And get in the cab and keep your ear on the radio, all right?

He turns and hurries toward the theater. Christy walks forward.

CHRISTY
Okay. Yeah.

JOHNNY
I won't be long.

Christy climbs into the taxi.

JOHNNY (O.S.)
(to Christy)
And lock the doors.

EXT. SIDE STREET – DAY

Johnny goes past stage hands as he opens a door that reads: "Stage Door"

EXT. STREET/THEATRE – DAY

We see Ariel clutching a radio in the taxi.

ARIEL
(into radio, to Controller)
Four-O-One to base. If you can hear me.

CONTROLLER
(through radio)
Hello, base here — Hey, where's your dad, girls?

ARIEL
(into radio)
He's in his audition.

CONTROLLER
(through radio)
Oh. Where are you?

ARIEL
(into radio)
I'm not positive. Christy, do you know where you are?

Christy leans toward the radio.

CHRISTY
(into radio)
No.

CONTROLLER
(through radio)
Oh.

Ariel moves to speak into the radio.

CONTROLLER
(CONT'D)
Are you on Broadway?

ARIEL
(into radio)
Yeah...

CHRISTY
(into radio)
Yeah, I think so.

CONTROLLER
(through radio)
Near where?

Ariel looks at Christy.

ARIEL
(into radio)
Near...

They glance around.

CHRISTY
(into radio)

Near the audition.

ARIEL
(into radio)
The aud...

They look at each other.

ARIEL (CONT'D)
Yeah, very good.

INT. HOSPITAL –EXAMINATION ROOM – DAY

Sarah seated on examining table, as a gynecologist checks her blood pressure.

SARAH
Is my baby all right?

He removes the stethoscope from his ears – looks at her eyes.

Mateo looks at the wind chimes.

EXT. STREET/APARTMENT BUILDING – DAY

Johnny opens the door of his taxi, climbs out.

> **JOHNNY**
> (to Christy and Ariel)
> Wow, youse look great. You'll knock 'em out.

Ariel steps toward him. Johnny moves to close the taxi door. Ariel looks at Johnny as Christy and Sarah approach.

> **SARAH**
> Can you guess what they are?

> **JOHNNY (O.S.)**
> (to Christy and Ariel)
> Ariel's an angel.

Ariel jumps up and down.

> **SARAH (CONT'D)**
> Uh-huh.

Johnny studies Christy.

> **GYNECOLOGIST**
> How are you feeling?

> **SARAH**
> Fine. A little bit tired, but other than that I'm okay.

INT. MATEO'S APARTMENT – LIVING AREA – DAY

Mateo cracks an egg into a bowl.

> **ARIEL (O.S.)**
> (sings)
> *Just call me angel in the morning*
> *Angel*

He hears the singing.

> **ARIEL (O.S.) (CONT'D)**
> *Just kiss my cheek before you leave*
> *Angel*

Wind chimes moving.

> **ARIEL (O.S.) (CONT'D)**
> (to Sarah)
> Mam, do you think dad will know who I am?

JOHNNY
Christy's a forest.

SARAH
(to Johnny)
She's autumn.

CHRISTY
No, fall.

JOHNNY
Fall?

CHRISTY
Yeah, that's what they call it here in America. Fall. Like leaves fall.

FRANK (O.S.)
(to Christy and Ariel)
Oh, you guys look great.

Sarah glances at Johnny.

FRANK (CONT'D)
They look great.

He turns to Johnny.

FRANK
Irish, Irish...

Sarah leaves.

FRANK (CONT'D)
...spare a quarter, please? Please, please?

Angela approaches from the background.

JOHNNY
I got a quarter.

Johnny hands a coin to Frank.

FRANK
You're the be...

JOHNNY
All right?

FRANK
He gave me a quarter, Angela.

Frank continues to walk along with Johnny.

FRANK
(softly)
Come on.

CHRISTY
(to passerby)
Hi.

FRANK
(to Angela)
He gave me a quarter.

Johnny hands a dollar bill to Frank.

JOHNNY
There you go.

FRANK
Thank you, sir. Thank you. Thank you.

Johnny hurries across the street towards Christy, Ariel and Sarah.

INT. SCHOOL HALL – DAY

Just beside St. Anthony's Church is the school assembly hall. When the family goes through the doors there are a thousand and one children all dressed up in expensive store-bought Halloween costumes. Christy and Ariel look completely out of place in their homemade costumes. All the kids stop playing and look at them.

1ST GIRL (O.S.)
(to friends)
Who are they?

2ND GIRL (O.S.)
(to friends)
That's the Irish.

ARIEL
(to Sarah and Christy)
What's wrong?

A girl looks at Christy and Ariel.

ARIEL (CONT'D)
(to Sarah and Christy)
What's wrong?

CHRISTY (O.S.)
(to Ariel)
Everyone else has bought their costumes.

CHRISTY (CONT'D)
(to Sarah)
We look stupid.

SARAH
No, you don't.

She places her arm around Christy's shoulders.

SARAH (CONT'D)
Come on.

She kisses Christy's head.

INT. SCHOOL HALL – LATER

Christy, Ariel, a boy and nuns stand at a table. A nun hands ice skates to a boy, he bows, then exits.

NUN
(into mic, to children)

And last but not least, a special prize this year... for the best homemade costume goes to the Sullivan children.

Ariel and Christy step forward. The nun hands a prize to Ariel. Ariel leaves, and the nun hands a prize to Christy.

CHRISTY
(to nun, mouths)
Thank you.

EXT. STREET – DAY

Ariel and Christy walk along a busy street, followed by Sarah and Johnny. Christy tosses the prize into the trash can.

JOHNNY
Ah, you can't throw away your prize.

Johnny takes the prize from the trash can.

JOHNNY (CONT'D)
Best homemade costume.

Christy
They made it up 'cuz they pity us.

JOHNNY
You got it 'cuz you're different.

ARIEL
We don't want to be different. We want to be the same as everybody else.

JOHNNY
Why would youse wanna be the same as everybody else?

ARIEL
But everybody else goes trick or treating.

SARAH
What's that?

ARIEL
It's what they do here for Halloween.

JOHNNY
What do you mean, like help the Halloween party?

CHRISTY
No, not help the Halloween party. You don't ask for help in America, you demand it.

CHRISTY
Trick or treat. You don't ask, you threaten.

SARAH
You can't do that on our street.

CHRISTY
Why not?

SARAH
Because you can't threaten drug addicts and transvestites, that's why.

They continue down a busy street.

ARIEL
What are transvestites?

CHRISTY
A man who dresses up as a woman.

ARIEL
For Halloween?

CHRISTY
No, all the time. All the time.

SARAH
(to Ariel and Christy)
Come on.

ARIEL
(to Christy)
Why?

CHRISTY
It, it's just what they do here, okay.

EXT. STREET/APARTMENT BUILDING – NIGHT

CHRISTY (V.O.)
We were allowed to go trick or treating in our stupid building.

INT. APARTMENT BUILDING – STAIRS – NIGHT

Ariel and Christy, wearing costumes, knock
on a door.

CHRISTY/ARIEL
(shouts)
Trick or treat, trick or treat!

The door opens to reveal Johnny.

ARIEL (O.S.)
(shouts)
Trick or treat!

CHRISTY
Dad, get out of here!

ARIEL (O.S.)
(shouts)

Trick or treat!

Johnny closes door. Christy and Ariel bang on
the door.

ARIEL
(shouts, slowly)
Trick or treat!

CHRISTY
Come on, let's try another door.

Ariel bangs on another door.

ARIEL
(shouts)
Trick or treat!

Christy bangs on another door.

ARIEL (O.S.)
(shouts)
Trick or treat! Trick or treat!

Ariel leans against the door frame. From up
above on the staircase Johnny keeps an eye
on them.

ARIEL (O.S.)
(shouts)
Trick or treat! Trick or treat!

JOHNNY
Answer the fucking door.

Ariel bangs on another door.

ARIEL
(shouts)
Trick or treat! Trick or treat!
(to Christy)
Why won't they answer?

CHRISTY
Maybe they're afraid.

Along landing, Christy and Ariel bang on
another door.

CHRISTY/ARIEL
(shout)
Trick or treat!

"The two girls were extraordinary, just amazing, almost miraculous in their naturalism. I wouldn't even call what they did performances, because they go beyond that. There really is a certain magic to them."
— Jim Sheridan

CHRISTY
(shouts)
Trick or treat!

ARIEL
(shouts)
Let us in!

CHRISTY
(shouts)
Trick or...

ARIEL
(shouts)
Hey, mister, we're nice kids, so let us in.

Sarah and Johnny listen to their kids knocking on their neighbors' doors with no success.

JOHNNY
(to Sarah)

How many doors is that?

SARAH
Four.

ARIEL (O.S.)
(shouts, slowly)
Trick or treat!

JOHNNY
Why am I so anxious?

ARIEL (O.S.)
(shouts)
Trick or treat!

SARAH
It's the stairs, Johnny.

INT. APARTMENT BUILDING, STAIRS – NIGHT

Ariel and Christy finally approach the door with "Keep away" written on it.

CHRISTY (O.S.)
That says "Keep away."

ARIEL
I don't care. Come on, Christy.

They stop by Mateo's door and bang it.

ARIEL/CHRISTY
Trick or treat — Trick or treat.

INT. MATEO'S APARTMENT - DARKROOM -
NIGHT

Mateo lifts a photograph from a tray, pegs it
to a clothesline.

INTERCUT/INT. APARTMENT BUILDING –
STAIRS – CONTINUOUS

Ariel and Christy bang on the door again.

ARIEL/CHRISTY
(shout)
Trick or treat! Trick or treat!

Mateo is annoyed.

MATEO
(shouts)
Who's there?

More knocking from the kids.

ARIEL
Tri...

Ariel looks at Christy.

CHRISTY
Someone's in there.

ARIEL
Oh my God.

They bang on the door.

CHRISTY/ARIEL
(shout)
Trick or treat! Trick or treat!

Mateo, from behind the door.

MATEO
(shouts in Spanish)

Other door.

On the stairs, Ariel and Christy again bang on
the door.

MATEO (O.S.) (CONT'D)
(shouts)
No drugs here! Other door.

Ariel looks at Christy.

ARIEL
Knock again, I dare you.

CHRISTY/ARIEL (O.S.)
(shout)
Trick or treat! Trick or treat!

MATEO
(shouts)
Who...?

They continue banging on his door.

ARIEL/CHRISTY
(shout)
Trick or treat!

INT. MATEO'S APARTMENT/STAIRWAY –
CONTINUOUS

The door opens a sliver. We see a white eye
warily looking at the girls.

CHRISTY/ARIEL (O.S.)
(shout)
Trick or treat!

MATEO
(shouts)
Go away!

Christy and Ariel bang on the door.

CHRISTY/ARIEL
(shout)
Trick or treat! Trick or treat!

MATEO
(shouts)
What?!

ARIEL

Hello.

Mateo looks at Christy and Ariel.

MATEO

You the kids from upstairs?

CHRISTY

Yeah.

Mateo looks down, scratches his neck.

MATEO

Is this Halloween?

CHRISTY (O.S.)

Yeah.

MATEO

Mmm. Where are you from?

CHRISTY

Ireland.

MATEO

You came all the way to America to trick or treat?

CHRISTY

(scoffs)

Yeah.

MATEO

Come in.

Mateo steps back – looks down at Ariel and Christy.

MATEO (CONT'D)

Are there only two of you?

Christy steps forward.

CHRISTY

Two girls.

Mateo presses his hand against the door frame as he leans through doorway. He glances around. Sarah comes out of her apartment doorway. She rubs her pregnant stomach.

Mateo stands in doorway glancing around. Sarah looks down at Mateo through the banister. Mateo looks up at Sarah, steps back and waves. He turns and goes inside his apartment. Sarah waves as Johnny steps through doorway. Instant trust.

JOHNNY

Are they all right in there?

(beat)

Are they all right in there?

She turns and looks at him.

>   SARAH
> Mmm-hmm.

She goes back inside their apartment.

>   SARAH
> They'll be fine.

INT. MATEO'S APARTMENT – LIVING AREA –
NIGHT

>   ARIEL (O.S.)
> What's your name?

>   MATEO
> Mateo. What's yours?

>   ARIEL
> Ariel. Hello.

>   MATEO (O.S.)
>   (softly)
> Hello.

>   CHRISTY
> My name's Christy.

>   MATEO (O.S.)
> Hi, Christy.

Ariel runs her finger over the painting.

>   ARIEL
> Is that our building?

>   MATEO (O.S.)
> Yes, it is.

Ariel looks at the painting.

INT. APARTMENT BUILDING – STAIRS – CON-
TINUOUS

Johnny comes out of their apartment, listening. His face blank, unreadable.

INT. MATEO'S APARTMENT – LIVING AREA –
CONTINUOUS

Ariel looks at the painting Mateo is making of
the building.

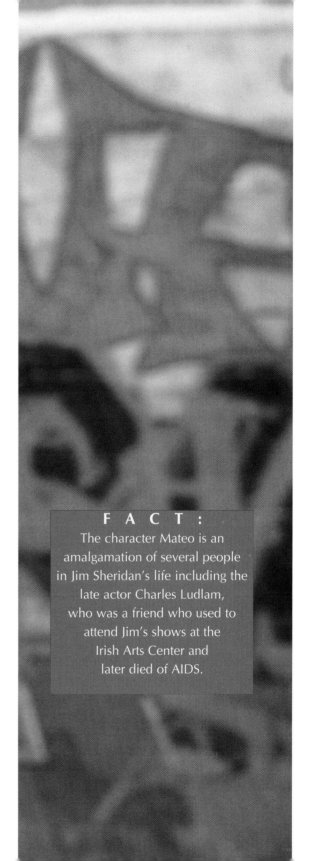

F A C T :
The character Mateo is an
amalgamation of several people
in Jim Sheridan's life including the
late actor Charles Ludlam,
who was a friend who used to
attend Jim's shows at the
Irish Arts Center and
later died of AIDS.

ARIEL
It looks like a haunted house.

MATEO
It is haunted.

Ariel and Christy turn to look at Mateo.

MATEO (O.S.) (CONT'D)
But it's not scary. It's a magic house.

ARIEL
Frankie believed in magic.

MATEO (O.S.)
Who's that?

ARIEL
Frankie. Our brother. He died.

CHRISTY (O.S.)
He fell down the stairs when he was two.

Mateo turns and looks at Christy.

CHRISTY
We thought he was okay... but there was something in his brain.

Mateo sits down.

CHRISTY (O.S.) (CONT'D)
A brain tumor. And for those three years it got bigger and bigger. It was malignant.

ARIEL
(to Mateo)
Are you crying?

Mateo looks down, tears stream down his cheeks. He seems to suddenly let himself go. To cry. He trusts the children.

ARIEL (O.S.) (CONT'D)
Are you?

Ariel places her hand on his shoulder to make contact.

ARIEL (CONT'D)
It's okay, he's in Heaven now.

Ariel glances down at another canvas.

ARIEL
Is that your hand?

Mateo turns and looks down at the canvas.

MATEO
Ah, yes.

ARIEL (O.S.)
Is that blood?

He turns and looks at the canvas.

MATEO
Spaghetti sauce.

Mateo picks up Ariel.

MATEO
Come here.
(beat)
I better treat you or you'll trick me, am I right?

ARIEL
(joyously)
Yeah.

Christy looks at Mateo and Ariel.

MATEO (O.S.)
Okay, let's find some.

Still holding Ariel, Mateo starts to look around in cupboards and places.

MATEO (CONT'D)
Let's see, er... So, what's in the fridge?

As he opens the refrigerator we sees shelves filled with medicine and pill bottles. Christy looks at the refrigerator, then up at Mateo.

MATEO (CONT'D)
Er...

He closes the refrigerator door.

MATEO (CONT'D)
Nothing.

He turns and glances around.

> MATEO (CONT'D)
> Nothing, nothing, nothing, nothing,
> nothing... Er...

He rushes over and grabs a jar beside the phone. It is mostly full of pennies and odd five-cent pieces.

> MATEO
> (to Ariel)
> Oh. How about this?

He picks up a jar of coins, shakes it. Ariel shakes the jar.

> ARIEL
> How much is in it?

> MATEO
> A lot. Mateo's fortune.

Christy looks at Mateo, shakes her head "no."

> CHRISTY
> No, it's too much.

> MATEO (O.S.)
> No, it's not.

Mateo puts down Ariel.

> MATEO
> (to Christy)
> When luck comes knocking on your
> door, you can't turn it away.

> ARIEL (O.S.)
> Happy Halloween.

> MATEO
> Okay, happy Halloween.

> ARIEL (O.S.)
> Thank you, Mateo.

> MATEO (O.S.)
> Bye.

Ariel goes out to the staircase and she flies by Johnny.

> ARIEL
> Hi, dad.

Ariel climbs the stairs. Christy comes out and sees Johnny.

> CHRISTY
> We're going to show mam what we
> got, okay?

He nods. When Johnny turns around Mateo is there. He looks at Johnny as if he can totally see through him. Johnny looks behind him as if there is something there. Johnny is unnerved.

> MATEO
> (speaks in foreign language)
> Hulumba Makela.

Johnny nods and heads upstairs too.

> MATEO
> (softly)
> Happy Halloween.

> ARIEL (O.S.)
> (calls)
> Happy Halloween, Mateo.

INT. SARAH/JOHNNY'S APARTMENT – LIVING AREA – NIGHT

Johnny, lying on the couch, stares at the TV.

> WOMAN TO MAN
> (on TV)
> If you can't talk, knock.

> ARIEL (O.S.)
> (to Sarah)
> He was really nice, and he gave us
> lots of money.

> WOMAN TO MAN
> (on TV)
> Knock once for yes, twice for no, do
> you understand?

Mateo's a very interesting man, one who has been rejected by his own family because of who he is, but then he finds a family with Johnny, Sarah and their girls at the last possible moment.
— Jim Sheridan

          ARIEL (O.S.)
How much does it add up to,
Christy?

          CHRISTY
        (to Ariel)
Two hundred and forty pennies,
twelve nickels and two dimes.

          ARIEL
How much is that altogether?

Christy leans against the table.

          CHRISTY
Three dollars twenty.

          ARIEL
Wow.

Sarah glances at them and smiles.

          SARAH
And he had nothing in his fridge?

          CHRISTY
Just medicine.

Sarah looks over at Johnny.

          SARAH
We should invite him over.

          JOHNNY
No way. He gives me the heebie-
jeebies.

INT. SARAH/JOHNNY'S APARTMENT – LIVING
AREA – LATER

Sarah places a dish on the table. Johnny
glances around, looks at her.

Mateo is seated at the table. He removes a
blanket from around his shoulders - leans
against the table as Sarah picks up a spoon.

          MATEO
        (to Sarah)
What is it?

          ARIEL
It's called colcannon.

CHRISTY

It's potatoes mixed with curly kale.

Mateo looks down at the dish and nods.

MATEO

Mmm.

Sarah, standing between Christy and Ariel, brushes her hands together.

SARAH
(softly)

Right.

She picks up a spoon.

SARAH (CONT'D)

Plates, please.

They move to pick up their plates. Mateo watches as Sarah spoons food onto his plate.

MATEO

Thank you.

They begin to eat. Mateo removes a piece of silver foil from his mouth.

MATEO
(groans)

Christy and Ariel look at Mateo, then clap.

ARIEL
(gasps)

Mateo removes a coin from the silver foil. He looks at it and smiles.

ARIEL (O.S.)

Wow.

ARIEL

That means you're gonna be rich.

She bounces up and down.

MATEO
(to Christy and Ariel)

Halloween is called the Day of Ancestors. When the dead come

back and you hear their voices.

CHRISTY

How do you hear them?

MATEO

You hear their voices through the men dancing.

CHRISTY

What do they say?

MATEO

Er... they complain.

Johnny looks at Mateo. He is jealous of Mateo's rapport with the children and it is almost as if he is seeing his old self in Mateo, before grief grabbed his soul.

MATEO (O.S.) (CONT'D)

"You don't pay attention to me. You don't feed me. I'm hungry."

ARIEL

Are they ever happy?

MATEO

When they're happy, you never hear from them.

Christy smiles. Mateo looks down, picks up food, looks at Christy, smiles – he eats.

MATEO

Oh.

Mateo again removes a piece of silver foil from his mouth. Christy and Ariel applaud.

ARIEL

You're magic. You're winning everything.

Mateo removes a ring from the silver foil. He places it on his finger.

CHRISTY

That means you're gonna get married.

Sarah picks up a teacup, looks at him. Mateo

looks at the ring on his finger, then at Sarah. He smiles. Johnny reacts, looks down.

INT. MATEO'S APARTMENT – LIVING AREA – DAY

> ARIEL
> (laughs)

Mateo clutches an African mask to his face. Christy shoots with her video camera.

> MATEO
> (mumbles)

Sarah, seated, her face painted. She toys with paintbrushes. Ariel and Christy pass in front of her, followed by Mateo.

> ARIEL (O.S.)
> Christy!

> MATEO
> (to Ariel)
> Who's there?

INT. SARAH/JOHNNY'S APARTMENT – LIVING AREA – DAY

Johnny walks in and stops, looking at a palette and paintbrush on the pillow. He picks up the palette and paintbrush.

> ARIEL (O.S.)
> You see that?

He turns and walks toward the voice.

> ARIEL (O.S.) (CONT'D)
> (mumbles)
> Oh God. Do you not think I'm bad, or are you just saying that 'cuz I'm good? 'Cuz...

> MATEO (O.S.)
> (chuckles)

You are.

Johnny stops in the doorway, looks at Christy and Ariel.

Ariel, Mateo and Christy seated on a bunk bed. Ariel paints an angel on the wall.

> ARIEL
> Am I doing the wings nice?

> MATEO
> You're doing great.

Ariel glances at him.

> ARIEL
> Really?

> MATEO
> (chuckles)
> Yes.

INT. CHRISTY/ARIEL'S ROOM – CONTINUOUS

Johnny looks through the doorway.

> ARIEL (O.S.)
> I thought I was bad.

> MATEO (O.S.)
> No.
> (chuckles)

You're doing great.

INT. MATEO'S APARTMENT – LIVING AREA – DAY

A black-and-white photograph of a young Mateo with his parents. Mateo puts the photograph on a table.

> SARAH (O.S.)
> Is that you in the picture?

> MATEO
> Yeah.

Mateo picks up photographs, looks at them.

> SARAH
> So, you were rich?

He raises his eyebrows.

> SARAH
> Is that why the angel has blue blood?

Mateo places the photographs on a table. He turns and looks at a painting.

> SARAH (O.S.) (CONT'D)
> You know, in the Irish language, the word for Black man is...
> (speaks a word in Gaelic)

Sarah looks at the painting.

> SARAH (CONT'D)
> But that really means blue man. But the word for Black man is...
> (speaks a word in Gaelic)
> And that means the devil.

She turns, looks at Mateo and smiles. Mateo looks at Sarah.

> MATEO
> You have us figured out, huh?

Sarah smiles. Glances down, sits back.

EXT. STREET – NIGHT

Johnny on a busy street.

JOHNNY
(to himself)
Set in mine heart, go to me
I've approved thee with mirth
And therefore enjoy pleasure

He walks across the street.

JOHNNY (CONT'D)
Set in mine heart, go to me

INT. SARAH/JOHNNY'S APARTMENT – LIVING
AREA/BEDROOM – NIGHT

The reflection of the TV in a mirror shows
"The Grapes of Wrath." We see Johnny's
reflection in the background.

MA TO PA
(on TV)
They can't wipe us out, they can't
lick us. We'll go on forever, pa,
'cuz... we're the people.

Sarah lies on the bed.

JOHNNY
(to himself)
Set in mine heart, go to me

Sarah looks at the TV and smiles.

JOHNNY (CONT'D)
I've approved thee with mirth
And therefore enjoy pleasure
Also...

SARAH
Johnny, come to bed. It's late, come
on.

Johnny glances at Sarah, then down at a
script.

SARAH (O.S.)
Put the script down now.

He places a pen on the table, stands. He lies
down by her, strokes her hair.

JOHNNY
You're happy.

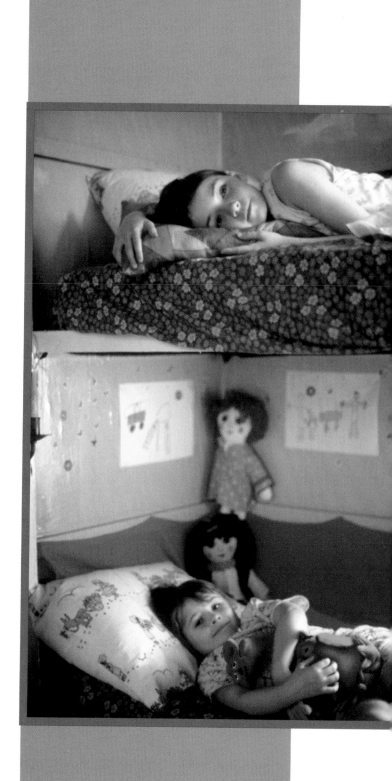

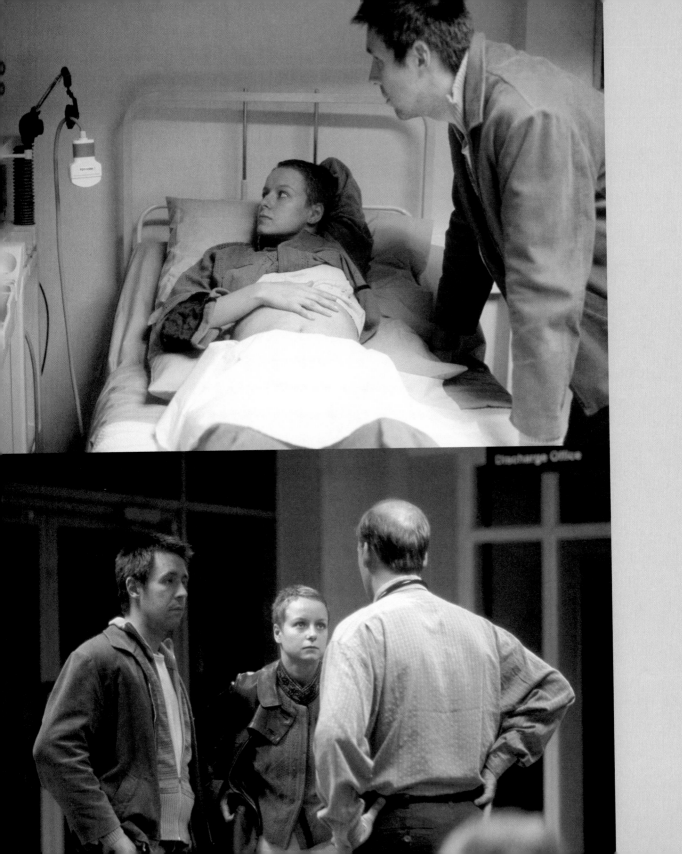

SARAH

I am. It's something Mateo said.

Johnny reads from the script.

JOHNNY

What's he say?

SARAH

He said everything's gonna be all right.

JOHNNY

Uh-huh.

INT. SARAH/JOHNNY'S APARTMENT – CHRISTY/ARIEL'S ROOM – NIGHT

Christy lies on the bed.

SARAH (O.S.)
(to Johnny)
And the baby will bring its own luck.

JOHNNY (O.S.)
(softly)
The baby'll bring its own luck?

Christy rolls back, strokes the angel painted on the wall.

INT. HOSPITAL – ULTRASOUND ROOM – DAY

A nurse gestures to an ultrasound screen.

NURSE

That's it, there. You see?

SARAH (O.S.)
I could be wrong, but...

Sarah lies on a bed. She looks at the ultrasound screen.

SARAH (CONT'D)
...I haven't felt the baby move for a couple of weeks.

The nurse moves the scanner device over Sarah's stomach. Johnny, seated next to the bed, looks at Sarah.

INT. HOSPITAL CORRIDOR – DAY

We see Sarah and Johnny seated on the bed. A gynecologist enters the room.

GYNECOLOGIST
It's serious.

He turns and exits.

INT. HOSPITAL – EXAMINATION ROOM – DAY

GYNECOLOGIST
This baby will not go full term. And if it did, it would be extremely dangerous to your health.

Sarah and Johnny look at the Gynecologist.

GYNECOLOGIST (CONT'D)
If you decide to go ahead with this... you'll have to be a very brave woman.

INT. SARAH/JOHNNY'S APARTMENT – CHRISTY/ARIEL'S ROOM – DAY

Christy and Ariel are seated on the bunk beds. They sit up and look at Sarah and Johnny.

ARIEL
(to Sarah)
But I thought the doctor said you couldn't have any more babies.

SARAH
Well, sometimes, Ariel, doctors are wrong.

Johnny is behind her.

SARAH (CONT'D)
(softly)
There. It just kicked.

CHRISTY
Oh my God!

Christy stands up, moves to pick up the video camera. Ariel looks at her. Sarah turns and looks at Johnny.

SARAH
Johnny, feel it.

Christy, sitting on the bunk bed, turns on the video camera.

SARAH (O.S.)
I remember the first time you kicked, Christy.

Through the camera lens, Johnny looks down.

SARAH (O.S.)
It was in one of your dad's plays.

Pull focus to reveal Sarah. Hold as she looks to camera.

SARAH (CONT'D)
Every time he spoke, you kicked. Like you were applauding him.

Christy aims the video camera at Ariel and Christy.

ARIEL
Did I ever kick?

SARAH (O.S.)
You? — You kicked like a mule, night and day.

Through camera lens – Johnny has his hand on Sarah's stomach. Zoom in as she places her hand over his.

SARAH
There it is again.

Zoom out as she raises her hand to her head. Johnny looks down.

SARAH (O.S.) (CONT'D)
(softly)
Johnny, did you feel it?

Through camera lens – Sarah, Johnny behind her. Zoom out and pan up to over framed painting of Sullivan family. The painting reads: "Frankie"

Sarah and Johnny look at each other. Johnny's hand is like lead on her stomach.

JOHNNY
I can't feel anything.

She turns to leave. Christy lowers the video camera, reacts. Johnny looks through the doorway to Sarah. He rubs his head on his sleeve, goes through the doorway.

INT. SARAH/JOHNNY'S APARTMENT – LIVING AREA – DAY

Sarah is seated – Johnny enters, she stares at him.

JOHNNY
Do you want me to lie?

She stands.

SARAH
So you're the only actor in the world who can't lie, Johnny? Not even for the sake of your kids?

They look at each other.

JOHNNY
What does that mean?

SARAH
If you can't touch somebody you created...
(softly)
...how can you create somebody that'll touch anybody?

JOHNNY
What are you going on about?

SARAH
(softly)
Acting, Johnny. And bringing something to life, it's the same thing. That's why you can't get a job acting, Johnny. Because you can't feel anything.

He shakes his head "no."

JOHNNY
This baby's not Frankie, Sarah.

Johnny reacts, wipes his face. The element of

truth in this wounds her deeply.

JOHNNY (CONT'D)
Look at me. Look at me. Why don't you look at me?

Sarah glances around.

JOHNNY
You've gotten over him.

She turns and looks at him.

SARAH
(softly)
I had to get over him, Johnny, for the sake of the kids.

JOHNNY
(softly)
So you're gonna put your life on the line for the sake of the kids?

SARAH
Yes.

JOHNNY
That's a total contradiction.

SARAH
How?

JOHNNY
You know what the doctor said.

She shakes her head "no."

SARAH
(softly)
I don't care what they said. What do they know about us? And my baby?

Johnny shakes his head "no."

JOHNNY
I gotta fucking get out of here.

He turns to leave.

SARAH
Where are you going?

She steps past him, leans against the door.

SARAH (CONT'D)
Where are you going?

JOHNNY
This is real.

SARAH
No!

He pokes her stomach.

JOHNNY
Right, this is real.

He kicks the door.

JOHNNY (CONT'D)
It's not a fucking play!

Johnny moves to open the door.

SARAH
What are you talking about? Where are you going?

JOHNNY
Just let me get out, huh.

SARAH
No.

JOHNNY
Let me get out.

SARAH
No.

He bangs his fist against the door.

JUMP CUT

He continues.

SARAH (CONT'D)
You'll upset the kids.

She steps back, he opens the door, walks through. She hurries after him.

SARAH
(to Christy and Ariel)
(calls)
I'll be back in a minute.

She turns and goes after Johnny.

SARAH (O.S.)
Just come back.
(beat)
Johnny, please.
Johnny!

Mateo leans against the door frame, looks at Johnny walking down the stairs, passing Mateo.

JOHNNY
(to Mateo)
All right? Everything all right?

Mateo turns and walks back into his apartment. He walks through the door, followed by Johnny.

INT. MATEO'S APARTMENT – LIVING AREA – DAY

Mateo watches as Johnny paces.

JOHNNY
The baby'll bring its own luck, will it? I'll tell you, the luck the baby'll bring – the baby could infect her... and two girls'll be left without their ma. So keep your trap shut.

Mateo watches as Johnny moves around his apartment.

MATEO
You don't believe.

Johnny turns, walks back toward Mateo.

JOHNNY
In what?
(softly)
God? You know, I asked Him a favor. I asked Him to take me instead of him. And he took the both of us. And look what He put in my place.

Mateo stares at him.

INT. SARAH/JOHNNY'S APARTMENT – CHRISTY/ARIEL'S ROOM – CONTINUOUS

Christy embraces Ariel.

SARAH (O.S.)
(calls)
Johnny – Johnny, come back.

Christy looks toward her mother's voice.

SARAH (O.S.) (CONT'D)
Johnny, where are you going? Johnny?

INT. APARTMENT BUILDING – STAIRS – DAY

Past the banister to Sarah.

SARAH
Johnny! Johnny, you're scaring me, come back.

Johnny continues walking down the stairs.

JOHNNY (CONT'D)
I'm a fucking ghost. I don't exist. I
can't think. I can't laugh. I can't cry.
  (he slaps himself)
I can't fucking feel. D'you wanna be
me? D'you wanna be in my place?

MATEO
I wish.

Johnny steps forward.

JOHNNY
Are you in love with her?

He leans in to Mateo.

JOHNNY (CONT'D)
Are you in love with her?

MATEO
No.

He leans toward Johnny.

MATEO (CONT'D)
I'm in love with you.

Johnny stares at Mateo.

MATEO (CONT'D)
And I'm in love with your beautiful
woman. And I'm in love with your
kids. And I'm even in love with your
unborn child.
  (shouts)
I'm even in love with your anger!
I'm in love with anything that lives!

Johnny looks at Mateo.

JOHNNY
You're dying.

Mateo looks at Johnny. He leans back.

JOHNNY (CONT'D)
I'm sorry.

Johnny turns and walks to the door.

INT. SCHOOL – HALL – NIGHT

On Christy standing on the stage – a spotlight

illuminates her. A nun is seated at a nearby
piano.

SARAH
  (sings)
Desperado
Why don't you come to your senses

Johnny holds a video camera. Sarah, seated
amongst the audience, looks at Christy.

CHRISTY (O.S.)
You've been out riding fences

EXT. STREET – NIGHT

A busy street, trees decorated with lights.

CHRISTY (V.O.)
...for so long now
Oh, you're a hard one

INT. TAXI – NIGHT

On Johnny as he drives.

CHRISTY (V.O.)
I know that you've got your reasons

INT. SCHOOL – HALL – NIGHT

Hand held – Panning up over the scenery to
Christy.

CHRISTY (O.S.)
These things that are pleasing you
Can hurt you somehow

Hand held – Continue panning to the nun at
the piano. Zoom in as she plays.

CHRISTY (O.S.)
Don't you draw the queen of dia-
monds, boy

INT. SARAH/JOHNNY'S APARTMENT –
CHRISTY/ARIEL'S ROOM – NIGHT

Close up on video screen – we see Sarah and
Johnny in Ireland.

CHRISTY (V.O.)
She'll beat you if she's able

Sometimes I think our entire lives are make-believe. This is make-believe. The air I breathe is make-believe. Just make believe you're happy, Johnny — please, for the kids.

You know the queen of hearts is your
best bet

Track back as they embrace to reveal
Christy's hand clutching the screen.

CHRISTY (V.O.) (CONT'D)
It seems to me some fine things

Past Ariel to Christy lying on the bed, looking
at the video camera screen.

CHRISTY (V.O.) (CONT'D)
Have been laid upon your table

ARIEL
That's Frankie's room.

Close up on video camera screen – we see
Sarah and Johnny in a garden.

CHRISTY (V.O.)
(singing)
*But you always want the ones that
you can't get.*

The screen changes.

CHRISTY (V.O.) (CONT'D)
Desperado

INT. SCHOOL – HALL – NIGHT

CHRISTY (CONT'D)
*Why don't you come to your senses
Come down from your fences*

EXT. STREET – NIGHT

Johnny is seen through the windshield of his
taxi. Track with the taxi as it travels down the
street.

CHRISTY (V.O.) (CONT'D)
*Open the gate
It may be raining*

INT. SCHOOL – HALL – NIGHT

Johnny and Sarah seated in the audience. He
glances at the video camera screen.

CHRISTY (O.S.) (CONT'D)
You better let somebody love you

Zoom in on the video camera screen.

>   CHRISTY (O.S.) (CONT'D)
>   *You better let somebody love you*
>   *Before it's too late*

EXT. STREET – NIGHT

Johnny walks toward camera.

                         FADE OUT

INT. SARAH/JOHNNY'S APARTMENT – LIVING
AREA – NIGHT

Sarah lies in bed looking at Johnny.

Johnny walks toward her. He lies down on
the bed and looks at Sarah.

>   JOHNNY
>   I'm just scared.

He closes his eyes.

>   JOHNNY (CONT'D)
>   It's gone. I can't make-believe any-
>   more.

>   SARAH
>   Sometimes I think our entire lives
>   are make-believe. This is make-
>   believe. The air I breathe is make-
>   believe. Just make believe you're
>   happy, Johnny — please, for the
>   kids.

EXT. STREET/THEATRE – DAY

Johnny stands in a queue of actors.

>   ACTOR
>   Now is the winter of our discontent
>   Made glorious summer
>   By this sun of York
>   And all the clouds that there are

Johnny looks up at the actors in queue as
they open umbrellas.

>   ACTOR
>   Dance to the lascivious pleasings of
>   a lute

Heavy rain falls.

>   JOHNNY
>   Oh shit.

>   ACTOR
>   Now is the winter of our discontent

Johnny pulls his jacket over his head, the
actor leans over and picks up a raincoat.

>   ACTOR (CONT'D)
>   Made glorious summer by this sun
>   of York

The actor moves to place the raincoat over
his head.

EXT. TAXI – NIGHT

Through the windshield and past Johnny, we
see a stockbroker in the back seat of the taxi.
He snorts cocaine, then sits back.

>   STOCKBROKER
>   So I'm a little high at the moment.

>   CHRISTY (V.O.)
>   Sometimes it seems like everyone in
>   New York was an actor.

Johnny checks his watch.

>   JOHNNY
>   Hey, man, you know, you mightn't
>   think it to look at me, but...

The stockbroker looks at Johnny.

>   STOCKBROKER
>   ...and I know I'm white and every-
>   thing, but I can rap.

INT. SARAH/JOHNNY'S APARTMENT –
CHRISTY/ARIEL'S ROOM – NIGHT

Christy is seated on the bed.

>   PAPO (O.S.)
>   (calls)
>   Help, somebody! Somebody call an
>   ambulance!
>   (to Steve)

Stevie!

Christy climbs from the bed.

> PAPO (O.S.)
> (calls)
> Come on, man. Stevie, somebody!
> Somebody help!

INT. SARAH/JOHNNY'S APARTMENT – LIVING
AREA – NIGHT

Christy hurries to the door. She stops as Ariel
joins her.

> PAPO (O.S.)
> (calls)
> He's fallen down the stairs.

Christy glances at Ariel.

> CHRISTY
> I think someone's fallen down the
> stairs.

> PAPO (O.S.)
> (calls)
> Mateo's fallen down the stairs!

> CHRISTY
> I think it's Mateo. Get your coat.

Christy unlocks the door as Ariel turns to go out.

EXT. TAXI – NIGHT

Angle through windshield at Johnny.

> STOCKBROKER (O.S.)
> (raps)
> Cuz I got mad words
> Maybe some you never heard
> I'm the supreme white wet dream
> Like Larry Byrd And Boston off and
> dropping threes And freeze
> I'm...Be crossing boundaries like a
> ferry

INT. APARTMENT BUILDING – STAIRS – NIGHT

Mateo lies unconscious on the stairs.

> CHRISTY (O.S.)
> (to Ariel)
> It's Mateo.

Christy hurries to him, followed by Ariel.

> ARIEL
> Will I get the lemon drops?

Christy removes her coat, kneels down by
Mateo.

> CHRISTY
> Yeah, and a pillow.

> ARIEL
> Okay.

Tony enters, clutching a dog on a leash. He
hurries to Mateo.

> TONY
> Man, Mateo. Did anyone call for
> help?

Papo enters, climbs the stairs.

> PAPO (O.S.)
> He just fainted, man.

Tony's dog looks at Papo.

> PAPO (O.S.) (CONT'D)
> Whoa, whoa, whoa! Keep the dog
> away man, keep him away.

Christy places her coat beneath his head.

> TONY
> Go down stairs, Papo, man.

> PAPO
> Stevie doesn't let me, he'll lock me
> out.

Christy tries to resuscitate Mateo.

> TONY
> That's 'cause you're a junkie, Papo.

Christy continues CPR.

> TONY (CONT'D)
> Go and get an ambulance.

PAPO
(to Christy)
Don't do that. Don't, don't do that.

She looks up at Papo.

CHRISTY
I did this to my brother.

PAPO
No. It's different.

Christy continues trying to resuscitate Mateo
– she thumps his chest.

CHRISTY (O.S.)
Come on, come on.

Mateo gains consciousness – Christy leans back.

CHRISTY (CONT'D)
(to Mateo)
Are you okay?

Sarah arrives in the building.

INT. TAXI – NIGHT

Johnny painfully listening to his customer.

STOCKBROKER (O.S.)
(raps)
Wrecks with necks
I flex my lyrical pecs
With Lee on the decks
We break through border checks
Of player hating mating
To multiply
To press our success
Take us down from the high

INT. APARTMENT BUILDING – STAIRS – NIGHT

Sarah is crouching next to Mateo on the floor,
leaning against the wall. Christy is with her.

SARAH
Are you okay?

MATEO
Can't seem to catch my breath.

Ariel returns – she places a pillow on the
floor as she kneels down.

SARAH
(to Mateo)
Just relax.

ARIEL
Mateo. Here.

Ariel hands a bag of sweets to Mateo.

MATEO
What are they?

ARIEL
They're lemon drops. They're
magic. If you suck on some, they'll
make you better.

Mateo turns and looks at Christy.

MATEO
Is that right, Christy?
(he smiles)

CHRISTY
Yeah.

Mateo takes a sweet from the bag, places it in
his mouth.

ARIEL (O.S.)
My mam takes them to help the
baby.

MATEO
(smiling)
Mmm.

He looks at Ariel.

MATEO (CONT'D)
(softly)
I think you saved my life, Ariel.

Christy smiles.

EXT. TAXI – NIGHT

Through the windshield, we see the stockbroker rapping.

                    STOCKBROKER
              (raps)
Only play to those that's for us
Let my point leak across with my
porous chorus
Let my shit get lit up
Like my rap was bore us

Johnny can hardly stand it.

                    STOCKBROKER (O.S.)
              (raps)
Yeltsin sinking and drinking vodka
proper
My shit's more underground than
Jimmy Hoffer
I'm exceptionally lyrical
Have you all going hysterical

                    JOHNNY
All right, that's it. Get out the fucking car!

Johnny opens the door and climbs out – the
stockbroker reacts.

                    STOCKBROKER
              (raps)
Expecting our...

                    JOHNNY (O.S.)
Come on, get out of the fucking car.

                    STOCKBROKER
What are you talking about? I was
right in the middle of a flow there.

                    JOHNNY (O.S.)
Get out the car.

He tries to pull back as Johnny grabs his legs.

                    STOCKBROKER
Come on. What...

We see Johnny dragging the stockbroker from
the taxi.

                    STOCKBROKER (CONT'D)
...what the hell is the matter with

you, you freak?

                    JOHNNY
Get out the...

                    STOCKBROKER
Where's the Bill of Rights?

Johnny pulls the Stockbroker completely out
of the taxi.

                    JOHNNY
Get fucking out!

                    STOCKBROKER
Get the fuck off me, you piece of
shit.

                    JOHNNY
Take your fucking handbag!

The Stockbroker walks around the rear of the
taxi. Johnny throws the briefcase at him. He
closes the passenger door.

INT. SARAH/JOHNNY'S APARTMENT –
CHRISTY/ARIEL'S ROOM – NIGHT

Ariel lies in bed clutching her ET doll.

                    ARIEL
              (whispers)
Night ET.

                    CHRISTY (O.S.)
Are you awake, Ariel?

                    ARIEL
Yeah. Are you, Christy?

                    CHRISTY (O.S.)
Yeah.

                    ARIEL
What's wrong with Mateo?

                    CHRISTY (O.S.)
Some disease.

                    ARIEL
Will you get it?

CHRISTY (O.S.)
What?

Christy lies in bed.

ARIEL (O.S.)
Mateo's disease.

CHRISTY
Why?

ARIEL (O.S.)
Because you kissed him.

CHRISTY
No.

ARIEL (O.S.)
Night, Christy.

CHRISTY
Night.

EXT. PARK PLAYGROUND – DAY

Ariel and Christy lying on the snow-covered ground, making "snow angels."

INT. TAXI – DAY

We see a man through the open passenger window and across the snow-covered street.

EXT. STREET – DAY

Pan through the falling snow to a car.

Pan to a hotel entrance – guests stand beneath the awning.

EXT. PARK PLAYGROUND – DAY

Ariel tries to perform a handstand. Christy glances toward her.

EXT. STREET – DAY

Pan through falling snow to a traffic light. It shows "red."

A man wearing skis in the street. Followed by a second man wearing skis.

INT. TAXI – DAY

Through the open passenger window to a snow plow. Track over it as it travels down the street.

EXT. PARK PLAYGROUND – DAY

Ariel seated on the ground – she shakes her hands.

EXT. STREET – DAY

The men on skis move down the street. Pan across the snow-covered street to Christy, Ariel, Sarah and Johnny, who is walking Tony's dog on a leash.

EXT. PARK PLAYGROUND – DAY

Christy and Ariel are seated on a sled. They slide down the hill, followed by Johnny and the dog.

EXT. STREET – DAY

Past taxis to Ariel and Mateo, walking, followed by Christy clutching a dog on a leash.

ARIEL
There's dad.

Johnny holds a coffee cup – he turns as a snowball strikes him.

Johnny hurries, with Sarah behind him, towards Ariel and Mateo – as he hurries, he throws a snowball.

Johnny dodges a snowball, throws the coffee cup in his hand away. He kneels down and grabs a handful of snow.

POLICE OFFICER
You gotta stop this, man.

Mateo throws a snowball at him.

ARIEL (O.S.)
Get him, Frankie, get him.

Mateo hurries off, chased by Johnny. He throws a snowball at Mateo, Sarah throws a snowball at Johnny.

Through a fence and across the playground we see Mateo running. He throws a snowball at Johnny. Johnny throws a snowball at Mateo.

EXT. PARK PLAYGROUND - DAY

They both move to either side of a slide. They throw snowballs at each other. This continues until finally Mateo slips. He walks to the swings and stops, leans against the frame. As he sits on a swing, Johnny approaches.

> JOHNNY
> You okay?

> MATEO
> I was just out of breath.

Johnny nods.

> MATEO (CONT'D)
> What was Frankie like?

> JOHNNY
> A warrior.

> MATEO
> Masselo Masela.

> JOHNNY
> What does that mean?

Mateo turns and looks at Johnny.

> MATEO
> A warrior who's not afraid to go to the other side.

> JOHNNY
> The other side of what?

Mateo points around him.

> MATEO
> This.

Ariel runs to them.

> ARIEL
> Hi, dad.

Ariel runs between them. Christy enters, clutching a dog on a leash.

EXT. APARTMENT BUILDING - NIGHT

Christy's point of view - The moon as a cloud passes over it.

> MAN (O.S.)
> (on TV)
> Ladies and gentlemen, we are not alone. Here on this little ball we call the earth...

Down to Christy seated on a window ledge.

> MAN (O.S.) (CONT'D)
> (on TV)
> ...we have friends among us.

INT. APARTMENT BUILDING - ENTRANCE HALL - DAY

Through the glass-paneled door, past Sarah, we see Ariel step forward and lean against the door. Sarah unlocks it and opens it.

> SARAH
> Don't be scared. He's not too well now.

> ARIEL
> Did he not take the lemon drops?

> SARAH
> I don't think they agree with him anymore.

INT. MATEO'S APARTMENT - LIVING AREA - DAY

Ariel walks forward, followed by Christy and Sarah. Sarah stops, looks at Mateo.

Close up on Mateo - he looks at Christy and Ariel.

Christy now sits on the arm of the sofa. Ariel moves, stops, looking at Mateo.

> ARIEL
> Why do you have sores?

A warrior
who's not
afraid to go
to the other
side.

Mateo looks at Ariel, shrugs weakly. Ariel walks over to him.

> MATEO
> (to Ariel, softly)
> If I tell you a secret...

Ariel leans against a chair.

> MATEO (CONT'D)
> ...will you tell nobody else?

Ariel shakes her head "no."

> ARIEL
> No, I won't.

> MATEO
> (softly)
> I'm an alien.

She turns to look at him.

> MATEO
> (softly)
> Like ET. From a different planet.
> My skin is too sensitive for this
> earth. The air is too hard for me.

Ariel thinks about this for a beat. Deep down she can sense what Mateo is saying to her even if she has to put it into her own way of thinking.

> ARIEL
> (softly)
> Are you going home like ET?

This is the first time Mateo has really confronted this. He is very upset.

> MATEO
> (softly)
> I suppose I'm going home.

> ARIEL
> (softly)
> When are you going?

> MATEO
> (softly)

Soon.

> ARIEL
> (softly)
> Will you say goodbye to me?

Mateo nods.

> ARIEL
> (softly)
> Promise?

He nods.

> MATEO
> (softly)
> Yes. I promise.

> ARIEL
> Mam's having a baby. What do you
> think we should call it?
> (beat)
> We're going to call it after you.

Ariel looks down – Mateo is asleep.

> ARIEL (CONT'D)
> (to her family)
> I think he's asleep.

INT. HOSPITAL – MATERNITY WARD – DAY

Track down and up along a busy ward.

> CHRISTY (V.O.)
> My mam had to go into hospital, so I
> thought about using my third wish.

Continue tracking, revealing Johnny.

> CHRISTY (V.O.) (CONT'D)
> But I had to be careful.

Continue panning, revealing Sarah lying in a bed. Ariel and Christy are by her. Johnny walks around the bed.

> CHRISTY (V.O.) (CONT'D)
> If the baby came too soon, the baby
> might die.

Hold as Sarah looks at the video camera – Christy adjusts it.

Writer/Director/Producer Jim Sheridan said watching Sarah and Emma Bolger embody his own daughters' pasts was eerie at times. "My daughters say that the reason I liked working with the children so much in this film is that it was just like playing with my kids all over again— except that this time they did what they were told! But that wasn't true," says Sheridan. "They conspired against me, just like in real life."

Naomi and Kirsten, 1982

CHRISTY (V.O.) (CONT'D)
And if the baby came too late, my
mam might die.

Down to the video camera screen. We see
Mateo being taken from his apartment in a
stretcher.

CHRISTY (V.O.)
You have to be careful what you
wish for.

Pan past a doctor, through an archway, to
Johnny, Ariel, Sarah and Christy. The doctor
walks in.

JOHNNY
Come on, kids, time to go.

JOHNNY
(to Sarah)
See you later, all right?

ARIEL
Bye, mam.

CHRISTY
Bye.

Johnny, Ariel and Christy turn and start to
walk away.

JOHNNY
Take it easy, love.

ARIEL
See you tomorrow.

SARAH
Bye.

CHRISTY/ARIEL
Bye.

SARAH
Love you.

They continue through the archway to the
door – Johnny leans over and opens the door.

ADMINISTRATOR (O.S.)
(to Johnny)

Excuse me, Mr. Sullivan?

They stop and turn to the administrator.

ADMINISTRATOR
(to Johnny)
We'll need that check by Friday.

JOHNNY
For how much?

ADMINISTRATOR
Five thousand.

JOHNNY
All right, okay.
(beat)
That's great. Thanks.

Johnny turns and ushers the girls out.

JOHNNY (CONT'D)
(mumbles) Come on.

EXT. CAFE – DAY

Johnny is seated at a table.

JOHNNY
(recites)
You know the situation.

The waitress walks up.

JOHNNY
(to Christy, recites)
You know I'm in trouble.
(he shrugs)
Come on.

CHRISTY (O.S.)
(recites)
Shut up.

Christy is also seated at the table.

CHRISTY (CONT'D)
(recites)
What do they tell you?

She looks at a script.

CHRISTY (CONT'D)
(recites)
They're telling you no.

Christy turns a page of the script.

CHRISTY (CONT'D)
(recites)
You either do the job or you get out
of town — understand?

Johnny nods.

JOHNNY
(recites) I understand.

Christy closes the script, pushes it across the
table.

CHRISTY
That was good, dad.

JOHNNY
Yeah, it wasn't so bad from you.

Ariel sits at the opposite side of the table.

ARIEL
You're gonna get it, dad.

JOHNNY
D'you think so?

ARIEL (O.S.)
Yeah.

Johnny smiles.

CHRISTY
Will we sell the camcorder?

He shakes his head "no."

JOHNNY
Ah, no — no. Don't be worrying,
girl. Everything's gonna be okay.

Christy looks at Johnny and smiles.

EXT. STREET – DAY

Frank walks across a busy street. Traffic
clears to reveal Johnny, walking between
Ariel and Christy.

FRANK
(calls out to Johnny)
Hey, Irish.
(beat)
Irish?
(calls)
Hey…. Hey, Johnny. Hey, Johnny.

Frank hurries across the street to Johnny.

FRANK (CONT'D)
Haven't seen you for seven days. That
means you owe me seven dollars.

JOHNNY
(to himself)
Oh Jaysus. Not again.

Frank catches up with Johnny.

FRANK
A dollar a day keeps Frank away.
Hey, I, I'm joking. I'm joking.

JOHNNY
I've no money.

FRANK
No… no, no, no, no, I got, I got
something for you.

Frank takes food stamps from his pocket.

FRANK
Here, here.

JOHNNY
What are they?

FRANK
They're food stamps.

Johnny gestures, shakes his head "no."

JOHNNY
I'm all right, thanks.

FRANK
Come on, come on, you helped me
out. I'm just trying to help you out
for once. Come on, take 'em.

Johnny looks down.

> FRANK (CONT'D)
> You can't take something from me?
> Take the stamps.

Frank gestures.

> FRANK (CONT'D)
> Come on, take the stamps.

Johnny takes the food stamps.

> JOHNNY
> Thanks.

> FRANK
> No problem, Irish.

Johnny takes Ariel's hand, starts to leave. Frank watches as Johnny walks away with Christy and Ariel.

INT. SARAH/JOHNNY'S APARTMENT – CHRISTY/ARIEL'S ROOM – NIGHT

Ariel and Christy lie in bed. Johnny pulls a sheet over them.

> JOHNNY
> (softly) Come on then. Tuck youse in.

> ARIEL
> Dad?

> ARIEL
> Who's gonna iron our school uniforms?

> JOHNNY
> Daddo the baddo.

> ARIEL
> Dad?

> JOHNNY (O.S.)
> What?

> ARIEL
> I need money for school.

> JOHNNY
> Well, I have that sorted. It's all right.

> ARIEL
> Okay.

> JOHNNY
> Okay?

> ARIEL
> Night, dad.

> JOHNNY
> Goodnight.

He turns to walk away.

> ARIEL
> Dad.

He stops, turns and looks back.

> ARIEL (CONT'D)
> You forgot to say Christy's prayer.

> JOHNNY
> I don't know 'em.

> CHRISTY
> I'll say it.

JOHNNY
All right.

He walks back toward them.

ARIEL
Kneel.

JOHNNY
What?

ARIEL
(to Johnny)
Will you kneel?

He shakes his head "no."

JOHNNY
(softly)
No – I'm not kneeling, no.

ARIEL
Mam always kneels.

Johnny looks at Ariel and winks.

JOHNNY
(softly)
But dads are different.

He smiles.

ARIEL (O.S.)
I want mam.

JOHNNY
Christy, do the prayer, would you?

CHRISTY
No monsters, no ghosts...

Christy glances at Ariel and puts her arm around her.

CHRISTY (CONT'D)
...no nightmares, no witches... no people coming into the kitchen smashing the dishes...

Johnny looks at Ariel.

CHRISTY (CONT'D)
...no devils coming out of the mir-

ror...

Christy looks at Ariel.

CHRISTY (CONT'D)
...no dolls coming alive... Mateo going home — Frankie in Heaven...

Ariel closes her eyes.

CHRISTY (O.S.) (CONT'D)
...the baby not coming too early or too late...

Ariel smiles.

CHRISTY (CONT'D)
...mam, dad, Christy and Ariel all together in one happy family... and all well with the world.

Johnny watches over them.

CHRISTY (O.S.) (CONT'D)
Amen.

JOHNNY
You're great girls.

He adjusts the bed sheets around Ariel and Christy.

JOHNNY (CONT'D)
(softly)
I'll see youse in the morning.

ARIEL (O.S.)
Night, dad.

CHRISTY (O.S.)
Night, dad.

He turns to walk away. Ariel lays back – the light turns off.

ARIEL
(to Christy)
How much does it cost in the hospital?

CHRISTY
Thousands and thousands.

ARIEL
Goodnight.

INT. SARAH/JOHNNY'S APARTMENT –
LIVING AREA – NIGHT

Johnny opens the refrigerator and places a
carton of juice inside.

JOHNNY
To be or not to be. Blah, blah, fucking blah.

He closes the refrigerator door, turns and
picks up a towel – Ariel passes by.

JOHNNY
Why, there'd be no...

He opens the oven.

JOHNNY (CONT'D)
...to stick my head in the fucking
oven and end it all.

He moves to take the tray out of the oven.

ARIEL (O.S.)
Where's dad?

Ariel looks at him. Johnny closes the oven,
looks at Ariel.

ARIEL
I want my dad.

JOHNNY
I am your dad.

ARIEL (O.S.)
You're not my dad.

Johnny looks questioningly at Ariel.

ARIEL (CONT'D)
I want my real dad.

Johnny nods.

JOHNNY
Come here.

He steps forward.

ARIEL (O.S.)
Stay away from me.

She steps back, looks at Johnny.

JOHNNY (O.S.)
Come here to me.

Johnny walks over to Ariel.

ARIEL
Where's my mam? What'd you do
with mam?

JOHNNY
I'll get mam. Come here.

She shakes her head "no."

JOHNNY (CONT'D)
Come here, baby.

She struggles as he picks her up.

ARIEL
(shouts)
No! mam, mam, mam!

JOHNNY
Come here.

He holds a washcloth under the tap.

ARIEL (O.S.)
(shouts)
Mam, mam!

Johnny holds Ariel and carries her to the table.

JOHNNY
Sshh, sshh. Here, sshh.

He wipes her face with the wet cloth. Then
turns to the tap again, holds the cloth beneath
it.

ARIEL
(shouts)
Mam, mam!

He turns and steps back to her.

JOHNNY
Come here to me.

Johnny squeezes the cloth and wipes her
face.

JOHNNY
Sshh, sshh-sshh, sshh.

ARIEL
No! Nooooo!

JOHNNY
Sshh, hey, hey, hey, look at me,
look at me, look at me, look at me.

He steps back. Ariel looks at him.

JOHNNY (CONT'D)
Look at me. Am I your dad?

Ariel looks at Johnny, shakes her head "no."

ARIEL
No.

JOHNNY
(softly)
Here, look.

He snaps his fingers, dances.

JOHNNY (CONT'D)
(softly)
Look at me.

He leans down to her.

JOHNNY (CONT'D)
Am I your da?

ARIEL

Maybe.

Johnny responds to this possibility.

EXT. PARK – DAY

SPEEDED UP

Pan down to a water lily – it opens.

CHRISTY (V.O.)

So spring came. And with it, the
baby. It had come too soon.

INT. HOSPITAL MATERNITY WARD – DAY

Sarah lies on a bed. She leans forward.

SARAH
(whispers, mumbles)
Be a little girl.

Sarah steps through the doorway, she clutches
herself. A pregnant woman enters, walks to her.

SARAH
(to pregnant woman)
Can you get Karen for me?

PREGNANT WOMAN
(softly)
Are you okay?

SARAH

Can you get Karen for me?

The pregnant woman turns to walk away.

PREGNANT WOMAN

I'll go get a doctor, sweetie, okay?
I'll be right back.

As she leaves, Sarah starts her contractions
and begins to crumple to the floor.

INT. HOSPITAL MATERNITY WARD – LATER

Sarah is seated on the floor, between a nurse
and the pregnant woman. She leans back.

SARAH
(to nurse)
Please don't let my baby come.

NURSE

No, look, we've got you covered
here, we've got you covered...

The nurse lies Sarah back on the floor.

SARAH
(sobs)
I don't want my baby to come. No,
it's too early.

NURSE

Take it easy. Take it easy. Don't
worry, we'll... doctor.

SARAH
(sobs)
It's too early! No!

The pregnant woman leans in to Sarah.

PREGNANT WOMAN

We're gonna take care of you.

Sarah sits up.

INT. HOSPITAL CORRIDOR – DAY

SONG
*And a time to every purpose under
Heaven*

Johnny strides in, pulling on a surgical gown.
Johnny rushes along with a nurse – he points
to a chair.

JOHNNY
(to Christy and Ariel)
Kids, sit there.

He continues behind the nurse.

2ND NURSE (O.S.)

Coming through, staff.

An incubator is being wheeled in, followed by
a pediatrician.

PEDIATRICIAN

I need a morphine drip.

SONG
A time to be born

A time to die

Christy and Ariel wait in the corridor.

> 2ND NURSE (O.S.)
> Careful.

Two nurses enter, wheeling in the incubator.

INT. HOSPITAL DELIVERY ROOM – DAY

Johnny runs in – he sees Sarah seated in bed between two nurses. The pediatrician is in the background.

> PEDIATRICIAN
> (to 4th nurse)
> Nurse, morphine.

> SONG
> *A time to plant*
> *A time to reap*

Johnny crouches by Sarah.

> SARAH
> Johnny, why's my baby not crying?

The pediatrician turns, steps toward her. He removes his mask.

> SONG
> *A time to kill*
> *A time to heal*

> JOHNNY
> I'm going, I'm going.

He turns to leave – the fourth nurse places her hand on Sarah's shoulder.

> 4TH NURSE
> You're gonna be fine.
> (to 3rd nurse)
> Oxygen.

The third nurses picks up an oxygen mask.

INT. HOSPITAL – SPECIAL CARE BABY UNIT – DAY

Close up on an incubator as a nurse's hands enter, lifting Baby Sarah's feet.

> SONG
> *A time to laugh*
> *A time to weep*

A doctor looks at Johnny.

Johnny steps forward, looks down at baby Sarah. He leans down against the incubator.

INT. HOSPITAL – CORRIDOR – SIMULTANE-OUSLY

Ariel and Christy are seated, waiting. Christy lifts Ariel's foot, places it on her knee.

INT. HOSPITAL – EXAMINATION ROOM – DAY

The gynecologist looks down at a form – Johnny is in the background.

> GYNECOLOGIST
> (to Johnny)
> We've stabilized her for now. But she will need a blood transfusion in the next couple of hours.

The gynecologist flicks through some papers. He hands Johnny a form. The gynecologist leaves – Johnny looks at the form.

INT. HOSPITAL – MATERNITY WARD – DAY

Sarah lying in bed as she opens her eyes, turns and looks at Johnny.

> JOHNNY (O.S.)
> (to Sarah)
> All right? Everything's gonna be okay. The baby needs a blood trans-fusion. We have to sign this consent form.

He glances down at the form.

> JOHNNY (CONT'D)
> The pair of us.

Sarah looks at Johnny.

> JOHNNY (CONT'D)
> Is that okay?

She nods.

SARAH
All the blood is bad. Mateo said all the blood is bad. You're not giving my baby bad blood.

She wipes her face.

SARAH (CONT'D)
You gave my baby bad blood. And that's why he died. That's why he fell down the stairs.

Johnny looks at Sarah.

JOHNNY
This is the new baby, Sarah.

SARAH
He tried to climb the gate. And he fell. Why did you put it up?

She stares at him.

SARAH (CONT'D)
Where is he?

JOHNNY
Who?

SARAH
Frankie.

Johnny looks at Sarah.

JOHNNY
Frankie's not with us, Sarah.

SARAH
You should have taken the gate down. It's your fault.
(loudly)
You should have taken the gate down.

Johnny – he shakes his head "no."

SARAH
You're hiding him.

JOHNNY
(softly)
No, I'm not.

Sarah tries to remove the intravenous drip needle from her hand. He takes hold of her hands.

SARAH
I want to get Frankie. I want my baby!

JOHNNY
Sshh, sshh. Hey. Calm down, all right? Sshh, sshh.

Sarah lies back.

SARAH
(breathes heavily)

She sits up, glances around.

SARAH (CONT'D)
(loudly)
Where is he? I want Frankie. Where is he?!

Johnny pushes her back on to the bed. He stands.

JOHNNY
Easy, easy, easy. Easy, now.

She gets more upset. He turns and looks to the door.

JOHNNY (CONT'D)
(shouts) Doctor!

Johnny turns and looks at Sarah.

SARAH
It's your fault he fell down the stairs. Don't let him take my baby...

MALE NURSE (O.S.)
Doctor.

JOHNNY
It's gonna be... It's all right...

Johnny turns and looks at a patient on the next bed.

JOHNNY (CONT'D)
(to patient)

Could you ring your bell there?
(to doctor)
Doctor!

DOCTOR (O.S.)
(to nurse)
Five diazepam. Get me five of
diazepam.

SARAH
(to Johnny)
Why didn't you take the gate down?
Why didn't you take the gate down?

The doctor places his hand on her shoulder.

DOCTOR
Five diazepam, nurse.

Johnny looks down at Sarah.

JOHNNY
It's all right.

SARAH (O.S.)
(to doctor)
No, no, no, no, please.

Sarah grows more and more agitated.

SARAH (CONT'D)
Please, I'm begging you, please.

JOHNNY
(mumbles)

DOCTOR
It'll be okay. Just calm down for a
second.

JOHNNY
It's all right.

The nurse enters, hands a syringe to the doctor.

SARAH
Johnny, please, please. No, no, no,
no, no, please, Johnny, please.

Johnny closes his eyes as the doctor adminis-
ters the injection.

SARAH (O.S.)
(to Johnny)
No, no, I want to see my baby.
Please don't take my new baby.

DOCTOR
(to nurse)
All right.

JOHNNY
I'm not taking her.

She nods.

SARAH
(whispers)
Okay.

JOHNNY
It's okay.

SARAH
Save my baby.

JOHNNY
I promise.

SARAH
Save my baby, Johnny, please,
please...

Sarah is growing sedated.

SARAH (CONT'D)
(whispers)
Please, please, go and save her,
please.

JOHNNY
(whispers)
I will.

She lies back.

JOHNNY (CONT'D)
I will.

Sarah glances around, looks at Johnny.

SARAH
(softly)
If the baby dies, just don't wake me up.

Johnny looks at Sarah.

INT. HOSPITAL – PRIVATE ROOM – NIGHT

Ariel walks in, looking at the doctor. Johnny is in the foreground, shoulders down.

> DOCTOR (O.S.)
> (to family)
> Er, there's only one other solution.

Christy is seated on the bed.

> JOHNNY (O.S.)
> What's that?

> DOCTOR (O.S.)
> (to Johnny)
> Are you O negative?

> CHRISTY
> I am.

> RECEPTIONIST
> (over P.A.)
> Doctor Joseph... to radiology.

Christy climbs on the bed. Turns and looks at the doctor.

> ARIEL
> (to doctor)
> Christy's O negative.

> CHRISTY
> (to Johnny)
> What if I have it?

> JOHNNY
> Have what?

> CHRISTY
> Mateo's disease.

Johnny shakes his head "no."

> JOHNNY
> That's not possible, Christy.

> CHRISTY
> How do you know, dad?

Johnny looks at her. He thinks about this for the first time. It comes out involuntarily.

> JOHNNY
> God won't let that happen to you.

Christy stares at her father.

> CHRISTY
> You don't believe in God.

> ARIEL (O.S.)
> I'm scared.

Johnny thinks about this. He looks at Ariel.

> JOHNNY
> Don't be scared.

> ARIEL
> Everyone's dying.

Johnny looks to the doctor.

> JOHNNY
> Will, will she survive it?

> DOCTOR
> Well, she can't survive without it.

> CHRISTY
> That's what the doctor said before they opened Frankie.

The doctor looks at Christy, then Johnny. There is a pause while nobody wants to make the decision.

> DOCTOR
> What do we do?

> CHRISTY
> (to doctor)
> I'll give her the blood.

The doctor looks at Johnny.

> DOCTOR
> Is that a decision?

> JOHNNY
> Christy'll give her the blood.

There is a female doctor in the background. Johnny looks to Christy. He recognizes her strength.

CONTROLLER
(through P.A.)
Unit thirty-two, we're just...

The doctor stands, glances at the female doctor. He turns and walks through the door.

RECEPTIONIST
(through P.A.)
...to pediatrics.

Johnny stands, steps toward Christy.

JOHNNY
(softly)
Are you okay, little girl?

He places his hand on her head. She leans back, removes his hand from her head. Johnny looks down, surprised.

CHRISTY
Don't "little girl" me.

She glances down.

CHRISTY (CONT'D)
I've been carrying this family on my back for over a year. Ever since Frankie died. He was my brother too. It's not my fault that he's dead. It's not my fault that I'm still alive.

JOHNNY
(softly)
Ah, Christy.

He kneels down to Christy.

CHRISTY
Mam was always crying because he was her son. But he was my brother, too. I cried too. When no one was looking. And I talked to him every night.

Ariel looks at Christy, glances at Johnny.

ARIEL
She did, dad.

Johnny looks at Christy.

Mam, Dad, Christy and Ariel all together in one happy family.

CHRISTY
I talked to him every night until...

JOHNNY (O.S.)
(softly)
Until when?

CHRISTY
Until I realized I was talking to myself.

Johnny looks at her.

INT. HOSPITAL – WAITING AREA – NIGHT

Johnny leans against a vending machine – patients and hospital staff are in the background.

NURSE
(to receptionist)
I'm looking for, er, the Sanchez chart. Er, do you know if that...

Marina enters, clutching a sleeping Ariel. She looks at Johnny as the administrator enters the room.

MARINA
Listen, I'll take her home, okay?

JOHNNY
All right. Thanks very much.

MARINA
No problem.

Marina steps away. The administrator glances at Johnny as she walks by him.

ADMINISTRATOR
Your check bounced.

She leaves.

INT. HOSPITAL – PRIVATE ROOM – NIGHT

Nurse's hands holding a syringe as she draws blood from Christy's arm.

CHRISTY (V.O.)
I sat there with my dad, and all the noises of New York disappeared.

She watches the nurse.

CHRISTY (V.O.) (CONT'D)
All I could hear was the blood thumping in my ear.

She turns and looks at Johnny.

CHRISTY (V.O.) (CONT'D)
But for some reason I felt happy.

Johnny looks at Christy and smiles.

CHRISTY (V.O.) (CONT'D)
I wondered if Frankie had felt like this.

Christy looks at the nurse.

The nurse looks at her and smiles.

CHRISTY (V.O.) (CONT'D)
Everybody looking at you like they were looking in a mirror.

A female doctor is watching.

> CHRISTY (V.O.) (CONT'D)
> And smiling.
> (beat)
> Except in their eyes.

Close up on the blood bag as blood trickles into it.

> CHRISTY (V.O.) (CONT'D)
> Did Frankie know he was going to die?

She looks down.

> CHRISTY (V.O.) (CONT'D)
> Is that why he kept nodding and smiling at us?

Johnny looks at her and smiles.

FADE TO BLACK

Hold on black screen

FADE IN

EXT. HOSPICE – NIGHT

A taxi door opens – Johnny climbs out. He closes the door, walks away from the taxi.

INT. HOSPICE WARD – NIGHT

Through the window we see Johnny seated. He looks at a nurse, then turns and looks at an unconscious Mateo, who is in bed.

> JOHNNY
> When he died I cursed God.

INT. HOSPICE – MATEO'S ROOM – NIGHT

Close up on Johnny as he looks at Mateo.

> JOHNNY
> And I told him, "You're not gonna see these snotty tears running down my cheeks ever again."

He shakes his head "no."

> JOHNNY (CONT'D)
> So now I can't cry. You know, I thought I'd — come in here... and you'd wake up... you'd hold me... I'd cry — and the kid'd be all right. Everything'd be okay.

Close up on Mateo wearing an oxygen mask.

> JOHNNY
> We need a miracle, Mateo.

INT. APARTMENT BUILDING – ENTRANCE HALL – NIGHT

Johnny walks through the front door.

> FRANK (O.S.)
> Hey, Irish, whoa.

Frank is sitting on the stairs.

> FRANK (CONT'D)
> Hey.

Johnny moves around him to climb the stairs. Frank places his hand on Johnny's leg.

> FRANK (CONT'D)
> Hey?

Johnny stops, looks at Frank.

> FRANK (CONT'D)
> You can't say hello?

Johnny senses trouble.

> FRANK (CONT'D)
> What? What's up? What's up, what's up, what's up?

> JOHNNY
> I'm sorry, man.

> FRANK
> I'm just, I'm just... A bad day?

Johnny nods.

> JOHNNY
> You could say that.

FRANK
Yeah, whole world had a bad day,
Joe.

Johnny moves to climb the stairs once
more – Frank again grabs his leg.

FRANK (CONT'D)
(mumbles)
Come on, Joe, Joe.

Johnny tries to shrug him off.

FRANK (CONT'D)
Give me a few bucks... Come on.

Johnny shakes his head "no."

JOHNNY
I don't have any money to give
you.

FRANK
I'm sorry. I'm stupid, stupid.

He stands, steps forward.

FRANK (CONT'D)
Stupid. I shouldn't be bothering
you. All right, I...

He turns and looks at Johnny.

FRANK (CONT'D)
Come on, lighten up, Joe. It's
gonna get better.

Frank playfully "boxes."

FRANK (CONT'D)
Come on, Irish. Fighting Irish.

He takes a step.

FRANK (CONT'D)
I'm coming to get ya.

Johnny turns to climb the stairs. Frank
hurries after him, holds a cutthroat razor
against Johnny's neck.

FRANK (CONT'D)
Just give me some money. I'm

not doing this for me, it's for
Angela. Come on — put your
hand in your pocket.

JOHNNY
Take it easy.

FRANK
Your other pocket.
(beat)
Your other pocket.

JOHNNY
You gotta be...

FRANK
Faster, Irish. Let me see it.
(beat)
Now.

JOHNNY
I don't know what it is.

FRANK
Get it out.

JOHNNY
I'm taking it out.
(beat)
Okay. There you go.

Johnny looks down – he pushes Frank
against the wall, bangs Frank's hand
against the wall. The cutthroat razor drops
to the floor.

FRANK
Okay, okay, okay.

Johnny stamps on the razor. Frank steps
back as Johnny aggressively stomps on the
floor.

FRANK
(mumbles)
Okay. All right.

Frank leans against the wall.

               FRANK (CONT'D)
        I just needed money.

Johnny leans back, looks at Frank.

               FRANK (O.S.) (CONT'D)
        I'm sorry, okay?

Johnny leans forward.

               JOHNNY
        (screams)

Frank cringes.

               FRANK
        Okay, that's enough.

He crouches, then slides to the floor.

               JOHNNY
        (breathes heavily, then
        exhales)

               FRANK (CONT'D)
        Stop it.

Johnny leans back.

               FRANK (O.S.) (CONT'D)
        I'm sorry. Joe, I'm sorry I'm sorry.

Johnny steps back – climbs the stairs. Tony is
walking down the stairs, glances at him.

               FRANK (CONT'D)
        Hey, Joe. Yo, we're still friends?

               JOHNNY
        Go to hell.

INT. HOSPITAL – SPECIAL CARE – BABY UNIT –
DAY

Baby Sarah lies in the incubator.

               CHRISTY (V.O.)
        We were waiting for the baby to
        show some signs of life.

Pan up over the incubator to include Johnny.

               CHRISTY (V.O.) (CONT'D)
        She just lay there and lay there.

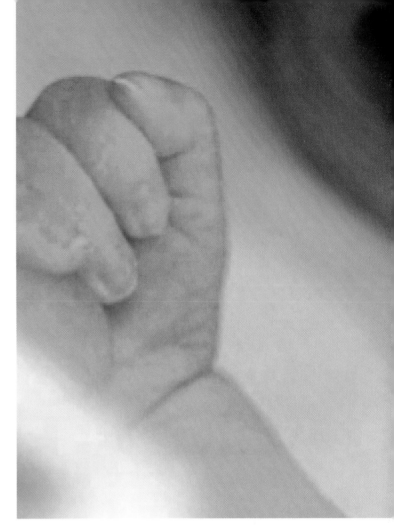

Johnny looks down at Baby Sarah. Sarah is
there too looking down at Baby Sarah.

INTERCUT/INT. HOSPICE – MATEO'S ROOM –
DAY

Mateo asleep in bed. A nun enters the room,
places a tray on a table.

               MATEO (O.S.)
        (speaks softly a foreign lan-
        guage)

She turns and looks at Mateo.

               MATEO (CONT'D)
        (continues to speak softly in
        foreign language)

Pan down to Baby Sarah.

> MATEO (V.O.) (CONT'D)
> (speaks in foreign language)

Close up on her as she opens her eyes.

> MATEO (V.O. (CONT'D)
> (speaks in foreign language)

Mateo opens his eyes.

> MATEO
> (speaks softly in foreign language)

Angle shot down on Baby Sarah.

> MATEO (V.O.)
> (speaks foreign language)

Close up on Mateo.

> MATEO
> (speaks softly in foreign language)

Down to Baby Sarah lying in incubator. Pan past Sarah to Johnny and Sarah. They look at Baby Sarah.

On Baby Sarah – Johnny and Sarah place their hands into the incubator. Baby Sarah clutches their fingers.

On Mateo – he stares forward, reacts – dies.

On Baby Sarah clutching Johnny and Sarah's fingers.

On Mateo – his hand is held by a man. The man lays the hand on Mateo's stomach, then sits back.

Close up on Johnny's hand. He takes his finger from Baby Sarah's hand.

Close up on Johnny as he looks at Christy. He turns and steps aside.

Close up on Christy. She looks at Johnny.

Close up on Johnny – he glances down at Baby Sarah, turns and walks to background.

INT. HOSPITAL – FINANCE DEPARTMENT – DAY

A nurse watches as the hospital bill prints out.

> CHRISTY (V.O.)
> The hospital bill arrived. It came to $30,420.20.

The nurse writes a note.

> JOHNNY (O.S.)
> (into phone, to agent)
> Look, just get me in the door for the audition.

Johnny clutches the telephone receiver, glances around and shakes his head.

> JOHNNY (CONT'D)
> (into phone, to agent)
> I'll give 'em whatever they want.

> NURSE (O.S.)
> Sir, your bill's ready.

> JOHNNY
> (into phone, to agent)
> All right.

INT. HOSPITAL CORRIDOR – DAY

An administrator strikes a key on a computer keyboard, looks at the screen.

> ADMINISTRATOR
> Hmm.
> (to Johnny)
> Bill's been paid.

Johnny looks down at the administrator.

> JOHNNY
> What do you mean?

Johnny leans forward in to the screen. The administrator looks at the screen.

> ADMINISTRATOR
> Ah, a Mateo Kuamey — paid it.

She glances at him, shakes her head "no."

ADMINISTRATOR (CONT'D)
There's no balance.

INT. APARTMENT BUILDING – STAIRS – DAY

Christy and Ariel are seated on the stairs, playing "patty cake."

CHRISTY/ARIEL
(sings)
See, see my playmate
Come back and play with me

CHRISTY (V.O.)
Finally, my dad got a part in a play.
And he came to tell us the good news.

Johnny walks down the stairs toward Ariel and Christy.

CHRISTY/ARIEL
(sings)
Since 1982

Johnny stops behind them. They stop and look up at him.

JOHNNY
Got some good news, girls. Sarah
Mateo Sullivan is coming home from
the hospital.

Christy and Ariel look at each other. He turns and climbs the stairs. Ariel stands, picks up her doll, runs up the stairs after him.

ARIEL
Cool, yeah!

Christy picks up the video camera – stands and runs up the stairs.

Christy shooting with the video camera – she walks back followed by Ariel, Johnny and Sarah clutching Baby Sarah.

Pan as they turn, walk forward. A door opens to reveal Papo's girlfriend.

PAPO'S GIRLFRIEND
Oh, look who it is.

JOHNNY
How are you doing there?

PAPO'S GIRLFRIEND
Hey, Papo.

They stop and look at Papo's girlfriend.

JOHNNY
(to Papo's girlfriend)
Youse want a look?

PAPO'S GIRLFRIEND
Yeah.

PAPO
Hey, look at that.

CHRISTY (O.S.)
What?
(refers to using her video camera)
Mam, can I?

Sarah nods.

SARAH
(to Christy)
Yeah, grand.

Christy aims the video camera, leans against the handrail.

SARAH (O.S.)
Don't worry.

Zoom in as Ariel kisses Baby Sarah – Papo's girlfriend, Papo and Johnny are behind.

PAPO'S GIRLFRIEND
(speaks in Spanish)

Tilt up and over Baby Sarah as she turns to look toward Sarah and Johnny.

PAPO'S GIRLFRIEND (O.S.)
Okay, see you later.

SARAH
Big yawn — big yawn.

Pan as they move to exit.

Christy turns and aims the video camera.

Ariel enters – track in as she turns and walks through the doorway.

INT. MATEO'S APARTMENT – LIVING AREA – DAY

Continue in and pan as Ariel walks to the window. Continue in and pan over the apartment. Tilt down to reveal Ariel seated.

> CHRISTY (O.S.)
> What's wrong?

> ARIEL
> He never said goodbye.

> CHRISTY (O.S.)
> What?

Ariel shakes her head "no."

> ARIEL
> He never said goodbye.

Christy looks at Ariel, lowers the video camera.

INT. SARAH/JOHNNY'S APARTMENT – LIVING AREA – NIGHT

Zoom in on a card, it reads: "A New Baby Girl!"

Pan down to a cake. The icing reads: "Sarah Mateo"

> PAPO (O.S.)
> (sings in Spanish throughout following montage)

Pan past a female and male guitarist, to Papo, his girlfriend – track up as Ariel walks in between them.

Continue pan as Ariel turns and steps away.

Papo reacts, gestures as a man offers him a bottle of beer.

On Ariel – as she eats, she looks at Johnny.

On Johnny – he leans against the refrigerator, looks at Ariel. She winks.

Pan to Sarah clutching Baby Sarah, and Marina.

Past Ariel to Christy, holding the video camera. Track in and pan as she aims it down at Baby Sarah.

Sarah comes in, looks down at Baby Sarah.

> SARAH
> (to Baby Sarah)
> Hello.

Down to a sleeping Baby Sarah.

> PAPO (O.S.)
> (continues Spanish singing)

EXT. APARTMENT BUILDING – NIGHT

Johnny walks to the window, lifts the curtain, stares out.

Pan across a darkened city to a full moon.

INT. SARAH/JOHNNY'S APARTMENT – LIVING AREA – NIGHT

Ariel lifts empty beer bottles from the table, places them into a bucket. Sarah holds Baby Sarah. Christy comes in, places the empty beer bottles on the table.

> ARIEL
> (to Christy, whispering)
> Sshh, the baby's asleep.

Ariel picks up the beer bottles, places them in the bucket.

> JOHNNY (O.S.)
> (calls)
> Christy.

Christy turns and walks aside. Ariel picks up a party blower and blows it.

EXT. APARTMENT BUILDING – NIGHT

Johnny sits on the steps.

> JOHNNY
> (to Christy through open
> window)
> Come here to me.

She climbs through the window, sits on his knee.

> CHRISTY
> Yeah?

> JOHNNY
> Look up there and tell me what you see.

She looks up at the moon.

> CHRISTY
> A full moon.

> JOHNNY
> And what else do you see?

> CHRISTY
> Stars.

> JOHNNY
> Can you not see Mateo?

She looks at him. He points.

> JOHNNY (CONT'D)
> He's going past the moon on his bike. I think he's waving goodbye to Ariel.

She smiles.

> JOHNNY (CONT'D)
> Will we tell her?

> CHRISTY
> Yeah.

She turns and taps on the window.

> CHRISTY
> (softly)
> Ariel.

Ariel appears, climbs through the window to them.

> ARIEL
> (softly)
> Yeah?

Christy sits on the window ledge, gestures.

> CHRISTY
> Look, look up there. That's Mateo

riding past the moon on his bike.

Ariel steps forward, leans against the railing. She looks at the moon.

> ARIEL
> (softly)
> Where?

Johnny points.

> JOHNNY
> There, look. Right there. Can you not see him waving to you?

Ariel shakes her head "no."

> ARIEL
> (softly)
> No.

He points again.

> JOHNNY
> Sure, he's right there, look.

On the full moon.

> CHRISTY (O.S.)
> He's there flying past the moon.

On Ariel – she looks up at the moon.

> CHRISTY
> Can you see him?

Ariel shakes her head "no."

> ARIEL
> No.

> JOHNNY (O.S.)
> Can you not see him waving to you?

Ariel turns and looks.

> JOHNNY (CONT'D)
> He's waving goodbye. Just like he promised.

She jumps up and down – waves.

> ARIEL
> Oh, yeah. Bye, Mateo. Bye.

Christy waves.

> CHRISTY
> Bye, Mateo.

Past Johnny to Christy – they wave.

> JOHNNY
> Yeah, bye, Mateo.

> CHRISTY
> Bye.

> JOHNNY
> Bye, Mateo.

Ariel looks up and waves.

> ARIEL
> Bye, Mateo. Look after Frankie, look after Frankie.

> CHRISTY
> Bye.

> JOHNNY (O.S.)
> Bye, Mateo.

Christy waves.

> CHRISTY
> Yeah, look after Frankie.

> JOHNNY
> Look after...

She looks at him.

> CHRISTY (V.O.)
> And then I asked for my third wish.

> CHRISTY
> Say goodbye to Frankie, dad.

Johnny looks at Christy.

> JOHNNY
> What?

> CHRISTY
> Say goodbye to Frankie.

Johnny looks at Christy.

Kirsten and Naomi with baby Tess.

INT. SARAH/JOHNNY'S APARTMENT – LIVING AREA – NIGHT

Sarah secures Baby Sarah into a push chair.

> CHRISTY (O.S.)
> Mam?

Sarah looks at Christy and Ariel.

> CHRISTY
> Dad wants you.

EXT. APARTMENT BUILDING – MOMENTS LATER

Sarah climbs through the window. She and Johnny embrace. He kisses her cheek.

INT. VIDEO CAMERA SCREEN

We see Mateo on a swing.

Ariel, seated, looks at Christy.

Christy is holding her video camera – track in as she aims it at herself.

> CHRISTY (V.O.)
> It was as hard for Frankie to smile when the tumor was malignant...

Pan down to video camera screen held by Christy. It shows Frankie in the hospital.

> CHRISTY (V.O.) (CONT'D)
> ...as it was for my dad to cry after.

She runs her fingers over the screen.

> ...but they both managed it. I'm going to switch this off now.

SCREEN SHOWS STATIC

> CHRISTY (V.O.)
> (CONT'D)
> It's not the way I want to see Frankie anymore.

She closes the screen.

Christy turns and looks to camera.

> SLOW MOTION

JOHNNY
(whispers)
Bye, Frankie.

Christy shakes her head "no."

CHRISTY
He can't hear you, dad.

Johnny stares at Christy.

JOHNNY
(softly)
Goodbye Frankie.

Christy stares at Johnny as tears fill her eyes.

Close up on Johnny. He closes his eyes as tears roll down his cheek. He opens his eyes, looks at Christy. She places her hand on his shoulder.

JOHNNY
(mumbles softly)
Get out of here.

He looks down. Christy has placed her hand on his shoulder as Ariel strokes his hair.

"And then I asked for my third wish.

Say goodbye to Frankie, dad."

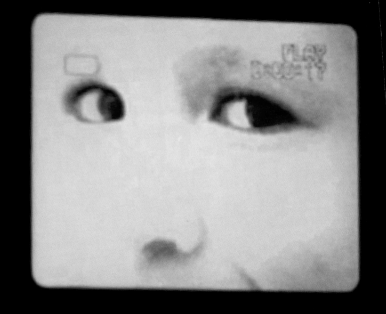

She closes her eyes.

EXT. NEW YORK – NIGHT

Pan across the bay to the city – a full moon in the background.

                CHRISTY (V.O.)
        Do you still have a picture of
        me in your head? Well, that's
        like the picture I want to have
        of Frankie. The one that you
        can keep in your head forever.
        So, when you go back to real-
        ity...

                        DISSOLVE TO

Full moon.

                Christy (v.o.) (cont'd)
        ...I'll ask Frankie... to please,
        please – let me go.

                        FADE TO BLACK

A Conversation Between Jim Sheridan and Annette Insdorf

Annette Insdorf, Director of Undergraduate Film Studies at Columbia University, is the author of books including *François Truffaut*; *Indelible Shadows: Film and the Holocaust*; and *Double Lives, Second Chances: The Cinema of Krzysztof Kieslowski*. She is currently writing a critical study of the films of Philip Kaufman.

Annette Insdorf: How much of your own 1982 arrival in New York to make it in show business can be found in Johnny?

Jim Sheridan: A lot. For example, even if it's hard to believe that a father would put all the rent money on winning a doll, I did. And I lost.

AI: You lost?

JS: Yeah, I lost.

AI: Wow. That's even more painful than the scene in the film, when Johnny keeps putting the rent money down to win the E.T. doll.

JS: Annette, the reality was so crazy. I got arrested—well, Fran was driving and she got arrested for speeding—but the judge thought it was me.

AI: You got arrested for speeding? When?

JS: When we came over the border from Canada. And the two cops took us to a midnight court. And the judge kind of lectured me and then said I could either plead innocent or guilty. I asked what happens if I plead inno-cent, and he said, "Well, I set bail." I asked how much, and he said, "I won't tell you." So, I said, well, I'll plead guilty. So, he said, "Okay, I accept it. You're fined $40." We looked in our bag: We had $36, and between the dimes and quarters, we made up $38. And then the police-men put in a dollar each.

AI: Was that in your original screenplay? It's not in the film.

JS: I could have put it in the original screen-play, but people would have been screaming that it couldn't happen! When we went out-side, the two cops said, "Our families were from Kerry, and we're sorry," and they gave us $10 to get juice. So, we literally arrived with no money. But I'd been doing a one-man show on Sam Beckett...I was going to get $400. All the facts, like carrying the air conditioner home, are true. I took the air conditioner out of the Irish Arts Center.

And our baby, Tess, was born premature. I was gonna put the reality of what happened in, but it was too difficult to believe. My wife Fran wrote a thank-you note to the hospital nurses, and they said that they were going to get rid of the bill because she did that. And that's even more sentimental and maudlin, you know. But a lot of the time in film, people won't accept that there's goodwill in life. Once you go into reality, sometimes there is goodwill out there and sentimental stuff that happens.

AI: In fact, you put more of that into the character of Mateo—the reclusive painter with AIDS who ultimately befriends the girls—and made him a formidable presence.

JS: Well, I made it Mateo because I had no way of finalizing his end. Mateo was a mixture of somebody I knew and the great American actor Charles Ludlam.

AI: Yes, from New York's Ridiculous Theatre Company...

JS: Well, he and Everett Quinton used to come to all the shows in the Irish Art Center, and we became great friends, you know. And then he got AIDS and he died very quick.

AI: I see how the film is personal for you, and how Johnny represents aspects of you. On the other hand, it's intriguing to me that the voice-over and the camcorder footage are from the perspective of Christy. For you, whose story is it? Did you feel that any one of the characters was more the "narrator" or subject than another?

JS: In a funny way, Christy represents me as a kid and Johnny represents me as my father. My character is probably the least in the film. It's because I had to split it in two.

AI: Sarah has quite an identity of her own as well. I don't want to short-change how she comes across.

JS: The first woman who reviewed In America said to me, it was good, but the wife was unbelievable. I said, well, you don't know Fran. She's eight times more unbelievable than this. And she put up with eight times more. But the trouble with characters you know is that you tend to make them saints. So, I had to find a way of keepin' her a bit edgy.

There have been some great films about true life, like The 400 Blows. But it has the distance of being a recollection. And In America doesn't have that distance. So I was stuck with a lot of the reality and, at the same time, four people who could tell me that what I was say-

ing was a lot of bullshit. I got the kid's perspective more from my own kids helping me with the writin'.

AI: In fact, I'd love for you to talk about the screenwriting process—not only how long it took, but the kind of input that your daughters, Naomi and Kirsten, had. Did they simply contribute their own memories, or did they actually collaborate in the screenwriting itself?

JS: I'm clever enough to get them to write a script and pay them a few bucks, so I'll actually control the copyright. It's not that I wanted to control their version of my life, or their version of their own life, but just to be fair, and to not have a lot of hassle. I asked them each to write a script. I commissioned them a long time ago to write their version. And it was very interesting because it was not at all like my version.

AI: They each wrote a specific one, or together?

JS: They wrote separate scripts. In Kirsten's, she was the hero, and in Naomi's, she was the hero. There's no other way of detailing the reality of your life. And I took quite a bit from both of them, especially into the childhood sections, which I didn't really know about. It was a way to get the kid's perspective on how idiotic the parents are—how the parents aren't as much in control as they think.

Apart from the pages about going to school and all the Halloween stuff, I got more of a feeling. And then I took their stuff and I put it into the version that I'd written, which originally was very sketchy and episodic. And even when I'd done that, I still didn't have more than a lot of charming episodes. That's when I made the decision to incorporate the underlying story of my brother. If I didn't, I had no way of making the story hold together. I had no mortar for the brick.

AI: So the decision to include your brother's death came later?

JS: Yeah, towards the end. It could have taken over the story, and I had to keep it balanced.

AI: *That leads me to ask whether the script changed much during the shooting. Here you are, the writer/director, including your daughters' input. But when you started shooting, did the script evolve differently?*

JS: Yeah, well, that always happens with me. It's both a strength and a weakness. I have a humanist perspective of trying to make the characters come alive. So I'll subject the visual to the spirit.

And I actually believe that cinema is not fundamentally a visual medium. It's an emotional medium and emotions are invisible. Therefore, it's the spirit that lives in the people, the thing you don't see. It's the same in acting, when you don't have to see what the actor's doing. In fact, if you do see it, they're overacting.

So, a lot of the time I think we do too much. And it's just about relaxing, doing less and letting it happen. I said in one context, the ultimate director would be somebody who's sitting there saying, "All these people will one day not be here. And I better give them as much freedom as I can allow them."

AI: *So the changes from script to screen during shooting were a kind of paring down, eliminating some of the scenes?*

JS: Yeah, it's always that. Anybody who makes films knows that you're always eliminating.

AI: *And then during editing, you probably eliminate even more.*

JS: Yeah. I just go on the set and I try to figure out what the scene's about and then do it. And I knew what the scene was about when I wrote it, and I'd usually written so many drafts, that I've done all the improvisation myself. So, if the actors are improvising, I have a kind of scaffold in my head of where they're goin'. I can allow them a lot of freedom. If they fall off the scaffold, I'll point it

out to them and say, well, that won't work in the story. And great acting is a lot about knowing where the story is.

AI: *How long did it take to write* In America?

JS: Oh God... I'd say ten years.

AI: *So many! And how did you and your daughters write together?*

JS: They did their main one draft, and then Naomi did a bit more before we started, I think. And then, once we shot it, we improvised again with Kirsten, and Paddy, and Sam, and the kids. There were things that weren't working and I had to find new ways of doing it. I would improvise with Kirsten, playing Sarah, which gave rise to a kind of Freudian joke: When somebody said to me, "Is it not weird having your daughter playing your wife?" I said, "Yes, it's weird having your daughter playing your wife, who's really your mother." How's that for a mess?

AI: *How old were Kirsten and Naomi at the time they wrote the draft?*

JS: Naomi was probably twenty-six and Kirsten was probably twenty-one.

AI: *So they had some distance from that childhood?*

JS: Oh yeah. I'd say Naomi's more the writer and Kirsten's more the director.

AI: *Did the experience of writing that draft for you feed their own screenwriting and directing? Was it a springboard for them to now have careers as well?*

JS: Well, Kirsten had already made her own films.

AI: *And they now have careers as writers/directors?*

JS: Yeah. Kirsten made her own film. Naomi is writin' a TV series.

AI: *I'd like to go back to one important point: you decided later on to incorporate your brother Frankie dying of a brain tumor. And I think his presence, or rather his absence, hovers over the film...*

JS: Yeah.

... the specter of grief that keeps Johnny from truly feeling. How difficult was that for you to write? Was it painful to incorporate Frankie?

JS: Yeah...

AI: *How old was he when he died?*

JS: He was ten, I was eighteen. I was about fifteen when he got ill.

AI: *Was including him in fact a good cathartic thing for you to do?*

JS: Well, it's very odd. I said to my brothers one day, "Everybody would talk about Frankie, but we keep driving around it." So I kind of wanted to, in a funny way, let it go.

The process of deciding to write about it is to be cold because you have to have an organizational level to what you're gonna write. Immediately you're into a manipulation of some sort. In neuro-linguistic programming, they get you to take a bad scene that you remember from your childhood and put film music to it, so you distance it. And this was a bit like distancing my own life. At the end I was going, "Is this my life or is it somebody else's?" So your own life becomes a kind of movie. You have a kind of weird distance from it. I think it'd be very powerful for people to do if they could afford it in therapy.

AI: *Getting film music is not so difficult.... Maybe Walkmans could help?*

JS: Yeah. The tragic memory isn't necessarily the one that you access as the most emotionally devastating. In fact, the most emotionally devastating events aren't conscious.

AI: *That's very true.*

JS: Loss is a thread with many writers and painters... Eugene O'Neill, James Joyce, and Yeats, for example. It's kind of like Van Gogh: They wrote a book on him called *Stranger on the Earth*, where the mother is in love with the dead child. So you have a kind of double grief: You lose the mother and you lose the brother. If I think of an idea, I usually try to put it up against the X-ray that is James Joyce. He was the only one with a good father, like Leopold Bloom in *Ulysses*.

AI: *Of course.*

JS: A Jewish man walking around Dublin was the only good father figure in Irish literature before 1980! And in Joyce's stories, the women were always in love with dead people: *The Dead* is essentially about that estrangement from the husband. And Molly Bloom is about the estrangement from the husband through the dead child. So, there was a kind of refusal by the women to engage on a loving or sexual level because of a death, which I always thought was probably like a psychological dramatization of the famine. So, I just stole a little bit from Joyce, and added the husband in love with the dead child. The attempt was to move the stone from the mouth of the grave, you know. To kind of get out of the death culture.

AI: *And come to America...*

JS: It's in the psyche of American people and the rest of the world that America accepted the Irish after their catastrophic famine. Without putting in the dead child, I had no way of accessing the tribal memory.

AI: *Sure. And, in a way, for me it connects to almost all of your films, which I see as exploring complex ties to both family and to place.*

JS: Yeah.

AI: *From* My Left Foot, The Field, *and* In the Name of the Father *to* The Boxer *and of course* In America. *Your screenplays (directed by others),* Into the West *and* Some Mother's Son, *deal even more with those complex ties to family and place. So, the dead child is in effect connected to both. That dead child is still in Ireland presumably.*

JS: Yeah.

AI: And there's a kind of mental tie to that past place. Of course, it makes the family slightly different as a unit than it would have been without the specter of grief.

JS: When I was about twelve, thirteen, we moved from a tiny little house, which was very lovely and quaint, to a big house. It was going to be a lodging house, where my mother was going to be a bigger slave than she already was with five kids, you know. And we were going to have lodgers so that we could go to secondary school.

AI: Right.

JS: So we moved from a genteel area to one that bordered a really tough area. The affinity with family is because probably it got lost in a funny way. My father was like the father of both families, the lodgers and us. So, you had a kind of non-nuclear family, which led me to believe nuclear families are like nuclear bombs... I don't know how people survive them!

The pressure of that huge nuclear family is almost too much for drama. People can't get out of it. Our family was so crazy with the lodgers. You know, I was like a pimp when I was twelve. I used to let girls go upstairs, to the lodgers.

AI: You could make a whole other movie about that.

JS: I could. I will....

When Mateo looks out the door for Frankie, that's when the film changes. I didn't realize it at the time, but by looking for the invisible, you force the audience to make visible in their own mind what they can't see on screen. It wasn't that manipulative when I did it, just emotional.

AI: Right. And in fact, you withhold the image of Frankie until the very end of the film. That wasn't footage of the real Frankie?

JS: No. But he had to get his head shaved like that for the operation. There was a little kid who had a shaved head, who we filmed. When Frankie was actually going for the operation, he got his head shaved and we came in after the operation. In the back of the bed is the doctor's report: my father picked it up and it said, "Too far. If I had opened him up, you know, drained off the blood...The tumor is deeper, it has claws. Go deeper....Drain off more blood, blah-blah-blah, go deeper. We can't go any deeper. If we go deeper, we kill him....I'll close him up." That was what my father read. So, it was this huge kind of...you couldn't even go there. It's so heavy.

AI: Yes. Actually, as long as you're on this, I would love to know more about your relationship to your own father because he was, if I understand correctly, a theater director in Ireland.

JS: Not exactly. When my brother died, my father worked a 9 to 6 job, and from 8 to 10:30 another job at night. He then decided he would have to go out and do things for the parish and the church hall, and he started a drama group and a disco.

It was almost like he was running out on the family, but at the same time, running into an imaginary family on stage. So, we would do "Shadow of a Gunman" or "Juno," and he'd probably direct it, or get somebody else to do it, and I'd play the malevolent son wantin' to kill him. We did a lot of drama like that, but I always wanted to push the drama group towards doing way-out stuff.

AI: Like what?

JS: Well, when I was about 21, [in] this little amateur group from the Irish equivalent of South-Central or the Bronx, we did *Dr. Faustus* by Christopher Marlowe. And it was wild. We had Pink Floyd music. I think my dad always wanted to be a director or an actor. He was very powerful as a presence, but he was kind of scared in other ways. My grandfather was a very strong IRA guy, you know.

AI: No, I didn't know that.

JS: And my father was the opposite. My father was Giuseppe Conlon [played by Pete Postlethwaite in *In the Name of the Father*]. My father was an Anglophile. He was kind of wise. But my granny and granddad were really tough. And you could get out of them that they'd been through hell.

AI: Is your father still alive?

JS: No, he died. This is a true story. I kept thinking, "Will I make a film about a good father?" and he'd be kind of nodding and having his pint. Because when I wrote the first play about him, called *Mobile Homes*, he was terrible in it. When my mother went to see the first production with him, I was sitting behind them, and all I could hear was her saying, "That's you. That's you." It contained little elements of my father, but magnified because of a child's perspective. So, eventually I decided I'd do a good father, and we did *In the Name of the Father.* On the night it opened, I said my mother was the prototype of the mother in *My Left Foot,* and he was the prototype of the father in *In the Name of the Father.* Pete Postlethwaite, who was playing him in the film, said to me, "It was a very emotional moment because he gave me a hug." And in my right ear my father whispered, "I love you." And I never heard him saying it before or since.

AI: That's very moving.

JS: Maybe everything I do is some kind of psychotherapy.

AI: There's such a fluidity, not only between the real experience and the fictionalization that you make in the film, but also within your movies. There's this fluidity between realistic and magical elements, between dramatic and comedic ele-

ments. I think of you as a kind of master juggler of invisible things.

To be more concrete, I loved the sequence where you cross-cut between Johnny and Sarah making love on a stormy night, and Mateo's "giving birth" to a painting with his own bloody handprint. And since this is the moment of conception, it's less hard to accept that Mateo's dying in the hospital—which you later cross-cut with the baby almost dying in the incubator—is what gives the child life. Was that juxtaposition already in the screenplay?

JS: It's a very good question. I have to write with the adrenaline of terror. I've trained myself to not write. I think the trouble is that there's too much writing in every script.

AI: Yes.

JS: You need to be on the edge when you write. Mateo was not as violent as Djimon. But once I had that inherent nobility and sensitiveness of Djimon—I consider him the John Wayne of black actors—I knew I could take him anywhere. I could push it and wouldn't lose the audience, even though they'd be scared.

AI: Right.

JS: So, the painting and the slashing the painting, the screaming, that was just me on the set going, "I know I need to have the character in the film before his door opens."

I've never seen painting work well in films. There's something inherently un-cinematic about a visual medium. Now, you can do it like Peter Greenway—kind of intellectual, a different meditation in the head—but I wanted an emotional moment. I was going, "This guy is gonna put his blood on the canvas. Like a painting in a cave." I wanted it to be totally primitive and, in a way, that's kind of me dealing with death.

AI: Was it in the editing stage that you decided to cross-cut this with the love-making of Johnny and Sarah?

JS: Yeah, that's true. That came in the editing. And that's a real difficult juxtaposition in the film there, with the kids absent.

AI: Right. In most of the other scenes, the children are present.

JS: Yeah. I believe the reason that we believe in the Virgin Mary is because we don't want to think of our parents having sex. There better be the Virgin Mary. But that concept of purity must come out of a deep need to believe we were conceived out of love. There's another part of the film when he's blindfolded and she doesn't know why she fancies him when he has the blindfold on. But she's brave enough to just go with her instinct to kind of save the marriage. There must be love in the blindness. I don't know what that means. But probably behind all the images and stuff, there is something very strange and powerful and...crazy.

AI: Yes. Nietzsche writes about the distinction between the Apollonian and the Dionysiac in The Birth of Tragedy. The Apollonian knows exactly who she or he is—very lucid—whereas the Dionysiac is drunk, loses the sense of self, and just goes with the instinct and the body. Maybe that's what a blindfold starts to give you. You let go of who you think you are.

JS: Yeah. Maybe you lose your boundaries. That's the role that drink usually provided in Irish culture. I often think that the Dionysian is attached to the hunter. In other words, the landed people didn't have the hunt, they probably slaved. So they had to have their Sabbath to stop them working. But then when they developed the vine, they went back to being hunters. The women loved that. It's like, "Oh God, we're back to being free. These guys are gone." It's kind of orgiastic.

There's a freedom for the women in the Dionysian male, even if he is going to be wild and sexual. They know he loves them. With the Apollonian puritan is the danger of being the warrior god. I don't know where that fits

in with this story, except that the woman is like matriarchy at that moment, making the sexual decisions.

AI: Right.

JS: Which I think challenges people in an odd way.

AI: And you have the storm in the background. It's not just primitive. Nature is somehow expressing itself through these bodies making love.

JS: Yeah.

AI: And Mateo making the painting during the stormy night—there's something Dionysiac about that, too.

JS: Yeah. In Shakespeare, the thunderstorm is always very important, right on the edge of madness. It's like the temperature builds to a point where something has to give. In the original screenplay that was more planned out. You could feel the temperature building and then going at that moment.

AI: I want to go back to this question of how you balance the dramatic and comedic elements, as well as the realistic and magical elements. I think of In America as being both, a sort of drama with many light moments through the kids.

JS: Yeah.

AI: How would you categorize it, generically? Were you consciously—in the screenwriting as well as the directing—trying to balance all of these elements?

JS: Once I got the kids into the hall, on the first day, and Emma looked up and the camera went down to her face, I knew she could be in the jungle as Hansel and Gretel. You know that a filmmaker is not going to damage this little kid. So I was carrying a fairy tale level. And I had to have the comic in there to stop it from becoming completely insane. Because I was dealing with real life, I was always on the edge of the comic—it could fall into stereotype. When you're dealing with children, you can go into stereotype very quickly; they'll pick up the emotion. The kids had to feel, "Jim totally knows what he's doing: he's playing."

AI: Was that difficult?

JS: It was really difficult to keep it light. That was the hardest thing I've ever done on a film—to keep it light, keep it comic.

AI: Actually, I'm surprised to hear you say that keeping it light on this film was the most difficult thing that you've done. I would imagine that on My Left Foot, *it might have been even harder to "keep it light." It's a heavy story that obviously does have some extremely airy moments.*

JS: Yeah, Daniel [Day-Lewis] in *My Left Foot* is kind of incomparable. I left the set of *My Left Foot*, after certain scenes, shaking and not knowing what I was doing. And this time I was kind of high in a joyful way. But it's probably easier to artistically control emotions like angst and trouble than to control joy. It's the element of joy that's so difficult for us adults to experience.

AI: For the joy to be expressed by an adult?

JS: Yeah. And once you go into a film, the reality of making the film becomes more overwhelming than reality itself. The crew and everybody begin to behave within the modus operandi of the script. So, say you have a script with an opening line—as the opening line of *In America* was once—"This is a coming of age story. . . unfortunately for me, it's my parents who are coming of age." It's where the parents were the children and the kids were the adults.

AI: Right.

JS: So that became the set. The kids knew that was the rule, that I wanted the kids to be in charge. I just think spiritually they'll do less damage.

AI: And maybe that's why you have the perspective from the voice-over and camcorder of Christy. She sets the tone.

JS: Yeah, it's controlled by her.

AI: And that was in the script as well?

JS: Yeah, but not right away. [U2's] Bono read the script and, a little bit unsure, wanted to say something. Meanwhile, I'd gone off and rented the camcorder. Bono came back and said, "What would you think of the kid having a camcorder?" It was weird! It was kind of like moving from an oral culture to a visual culture.

AI: Exactly. I do see this happening, especially among younger people. Whereas we used to document ourselves by writing diaries or letters to each other, now it's all become technologically mediated: We're all shooting one another, with our camcorders and our digital cameras. And that's how we leave a record of our lives.

JS: Yeah.

AI: I would like to talk about the casting—how you cast Paddy Considine, Samantha Morton, Djimon Hounsou, and the children Emma and Sarah Bolger—and how you directed the girls.

JS: Well, from the point of view of casting, I saw Samantha Morton in *Under the Skin*, and thought she was amazing. I saw Paddy in *A Room for Romeo Brass,* met him, and thought he was great. I went in to audition 300 kids and I saw this little girl, Emma, and I gave her the script. She read for Ariel and I thought she was too good, too confident. So, I went down to another kid and I gave her the script. She was only halfway through the fourth sentence when my coat was yanked from behind by Emma, looking at me. She said, "Jim?" And I said, "Yeah?" She was looking at me with pity, as if I crossed a line of etiquette that I wasn't aware of. She said, "Is she reading my part?" I literally stared at her to see if she was being tough. And she wasn't being tough, just...somewhere true.

In my head I said, I can't lie to this kid because I'll lose her. So, I said, "Mmm," and I waited, and I kept staring at her, and she didn't look away. After about thirty seconds, I said, "No, nobody's reading your part. You're cast." So, she said, "Well, my sister's downstairs," and I said, "What age?" And she said, "Eleven." I said, "It's a fourteen-year-old part." And she said, "Well, come down and see her." And I went down and met her, and drove around with them for fifteen minutes, and then said, "Okay, I'll rewrite it." But I didn't need to.

And then on the first day of shooting, something went wrong and I said, "Fuck." And the eleven-year-old said, "Can I have a word?" She took three steps away from the crew and said, "Jim, it's okay to cuss in front of me, I'm eleven. But my sister's six and it's rude to cuss in front of her. So, I'm going to have to ask you to stop."

AI: It sounds like your shooting was as fascinating as the story.

Lastly, you know which scene I liked best, although I found it excruciating to watch? The street fair, where Johnny throws balls to win the E.T. doll. Because the bet had to be doubled each time he missed, and it was all their rent money he was losing, I couldn't bear to watch. I had to look away because it was so upsetting to me!

JS: It's weird isn't it? A little game.

AI: You directed it so well that the scene had a greater emotional violence than most movies with murders or attacks.

JS: Well, I began to believe that God was on our side when we shot that scene, because we shot it in late October, after midnight, in Dublin, and it had to be over 65 degrees. And it's never been 65 after midnight, not in ten years. We kept thinking, "How are we going to do this? With heaters?" But I think God was on our side.

biographies

FILMMAKERS
JIM SHERIDAN (Writer/Director)

Writer, director, and producer Jim Sheridan's films have achieved popular and critical acclaim throughout the world and have garnered two Academy Awards for their actors, as well as thirteen Academy Award nominations and numerous prestigious international awards. With his fifth film as a writer/director/producer, Sheridan presents his most personal and magical story yet, the tale of a family finding its soul, *In America*, which he co-wrote with his daughters Naomi Sheridan & Kirsten Sheridan. Based on his own experiences coming to New York as a flat-broke immigrant, as well as remembrances of a devastating family tragedy, *In America* confronts the mysterious nature of love, loss, and finding new hope. The cast includes Academy Award nominee for *Sweet and Lowdown* Samantha Morton (*Minority Report*), Paddy Considine (*24 Hour Party People*), Djimon Hounsou (*Amistad*, *Gladiator*), and sisters Sarah Bolger (*A Love Divided*) and Emma Bolger in her feature film debut.

Embraced by international audiences, Jim Sheridan has nevertheless remained quintessentially Irish. He first drew worldwide attention in 1989 for his debut feature film, *My Left Foot*, which was based on the surprisingly uplifting life of the Irish writer/painter Christy Brown, a man with such severe cerebral palsy who could only move his left foot. The film's critical and box-office success kick-started a renaissance of Irish filmmaking and earned an amazing five Academy Award nominations including Best Picture.

Daniel Day Lewis was propelled to global stardom and the film marked the beginning of a fruitful collaboration between Lewis and Sheridan. *My Left Foot* went on to earn both Lewis and Brenda Fricker Academy Awards (for Best Actor and Best Supporting Actress) and received multiple Oscar nominations for Sheridan, including those for Best Director and Best Adapted Screenplay. The film also won the Donatello (Italian Oscar equivalent) for Best Foreign Film, among many other international awards and earned Sheridan a Writer's Guild of America nomination.

Despite numerous offers from Hollywood, Sheridan decided to remain in Ireland to direct his next feature, *The Field*, featuring an Oscar-nominated performance from Richard Harris as a farmer who vigilantly defends his land from real-estate developers. Sheridan also wrote the screenplay for the critically acclaimed modern fairy tale *Into the West*, directed by Mike Newell, which introduced the world to his more magical side with a story of the Irish traveling community (gypsies) and their enchanted white horse that seamlessly merged reality with fantasy.

In 1993, Sheridan wrote, produced, and directed *In the Name of the Father*, a powerful drama that recounts the struggle of Gerry Conlon, a man wrongly prosecuted and imprisoned for an IRA bombing, starring Daniel Day-Lewis and Emma Thompson. Drawing both controversy and praise for its searing realism, the film won the Golden Bear at the Berlin Film Festival and went on to receive seven Academy Award nominations, including those for Best Director, Best Adapted Screenplay,

and Best Picture. *In the Name of the Father* also brought Sheridan a second Donatello for Best Foreign Film and another WGA Award nomination. His next film, which Sheridan wrote, produced, and directed, *The Boxer*, reunited the director with actor Daniel Day-Lewis in a love story set against the explosive atmosphere of Northern Ireland. *The Boxer* received the Best Foreign Film at Spain's Goya Awards and earned Sheridan a Golden Globe nomination as Best Director. Sheridan also wrote and produced *Some Mother's Son*, directed by Terry George and produced *Agnes Browne*, which was directed by and starred Anjelica Huston.

Under his Hell's Kitchen banner, Sheridan has executive produced three distinctive Irish films: *Borstal Boy* about Irish writer Brendan Behan and directed by Sheridan's brother Peter Sheridan; John Carney's teen drama *On the Edge*; and most recently, the award-winning docu-drama *Bloody Sunday*, directed by Paul Greengrass, which garnered the coveted Audience Award at the 2002 Sundance Film Festival, the Golden Bear at the Berlin Film Festival, and two British Independent Film Awards, among other accolades.

Sheridan grew up in Ireland, where his brother Frankie died of a brain tumor, one of the real-life events woven into *In America*. Later, he began his career on stage, co-founding Dublin's Project Art Centre. He had numerous plays produced in Ireland, including the highly regarded "Spike in the First World War," based on Jaroslev Hasek's novel *The Good Soldier Schweik*. He was awarded the Macauley Fellowship for writers, and was at that time only the second playwright ever to receive the honor.

As an actor, Sheridan has also played substantial roles in two films by the Irish director Mary McGuckian—*The Words Upon the Window Pane*, in which he played the leading role of Dean Swift, and *The Bridge of San Luis Rey*, which was shot earlier this year in Spain with Robert de Niro, Harvey Keitel, and Kathy Bates. Sheridan played the role of the king of Spain in the film, which is set for release early 2004.

In 1981, Sheridan journeyed across the ocean to America, via Canada, to attempt to make it on the New York stage, with his wife and two daughters in tow (a third daughter was born in New York)—events which inspired the story of *In America*. While in New York, Sheridan received his only formal training in film, enrolling in NYU Film School for six weeks. He ended up serving as artistic director of the Irish Arts Center, where his creative leadership helped to win the theatre a 1987 Obie Award for "sustained excellence." Two decades after he first came to America, Sheridan came full circle, returning to New York to shoot *In America*.

FILMOGRAPHY

Producer

In America	2002
Bloody Sunday	2002
On the Edge	2000
Borstal Boy	2000
Agnes Browne	1999
The Boxer	1997
Some Mother's Son	1996
In the Name of the Father	1993

Writer

In America	2002
The Boxer	1997
Some Mother's Son	1996
In the Name of the Father	1993
Into the West	1992
The Field	1990
My Left Foot	1989

Director

In America	2002
The Boxer	1997
In the Name of the Father	1993
The Field	1990
My Left Foot	1989

Actor

The General	1998

NAOMI SHERIDAN (Writer)

In addition to *In America*, Naomi Sheridan has written two feature films, one of which she will direct in 2003, and is presently completing her third. She is currently editing a documentary, which she also directed, about the Irish soccer team at the 2002 World Cup. After working at the City Arts Centre in Dublin, Naomi Sheridan moved to New York to pursue her writing/directing career in 2000 and studied film production at the New York Film Academy in 2001. She has worked in the film industry in various positions from script advisor to production before writing and directing her own short film. Naomi Sheridan is the daughter of writer/director Jim Sheridan.

KIRSTEN SHERIDAN (Writer)

Kirsten Sheridan's first feature length screenplay, *Honor Bright*, won the Miramax Best Irish Screenplay Award '98. She subsequently penned the screenplays for the short film *Patterns*, which she also produced, edited, and directed; and *In America*, which she wrote with her father Jim Sheridan and sister Naomi Sheridan. She is currently writing two feature films: *Freedom, California*, and *The Olga Korbut Story*, and is directing a documentary series *7 Up in Ireland*.

Sheridan directed her first feature film, *Disco Pigs*, starring Cillian Murphy (*28 Days Later*), in May 2000. The film, which premiered at the Berlin Film Festival in 2001, earned Sheridan the distinction of being one of three finalists in Europe for the Sundance/NHK International Filmmakers' Award. *Disco Pigs* received critical acclaim in the UK/Ireland when it was released in October/November 2001 and was awarded the jury prize at the Castellinaria Youth Film Festival, the Gold Medal at the Giffoni Film Festival, the Grand Prize Best Film at the Ourense Film Festival and the Audience Award and Best Feature Film Award at the Young European Cinema Festival.

Sheridan has directed a total of five short films: the aforementioned *Patterns*, *The Case of Majella McGinty*, as well as *The Bench*, which she also wrote and edited, *Gentleman Caller*, and *Walking into Mirrors*, which she edited. Sheridan also was an editor on the short documentary *Ward Zone*.

Sheridan's personal awards include the 1998 Film Institute of Ireland/Guiness Outstanding Young Irish Talent Award and the United International Pictures Best Director Award 2002. Sheridan also recently directed a Druid Debut play "Abeyance." She graduated with distinction in 1998 from Dun Laoghaire Institute of Art, Design and Technology's film program.

ARTHUR LAPPIN (Producer)

Arthur Lappin has been a leading theatre and stage producer in Ireland for seventeen years, following a career as Drama and Dance director of the Irish Arts Council. He has produced twelve feature films, two TV drama series and several documentaries in this time as well as over twenty stage productions.

In addition to producing *In America*, his collaborations with Jim Sheridan include: line producer on *My Left Foot* and *The Field* and co-producer of *In the Name of the Father*. Lappin also produced *Some Mother's Son*, *The Boxer*, *Agnes Browne*, *Borstal Boy,* and *On the Edge*. He served as executive producer on the international award-winner *Bloody Sunday*. He was executive producer of *Laws of Attraction*, directed by Peter Howitt and starring Pierce Brosnan and Julianne Moore, which was shot in Ireland and New York in 2003 and will be released in 2004. He is currently in pre-production for a feature film *Omagh*, which is written by Paul Greengrass and being directed by Peter Travis.

Lappin is managing director of Hell's Kitchen, the production company he established in 1992 with Jim Sheridan. He was founding Chairman of Ireland's National Training Committee for Film and Television (now called Screen Training Ireland) and is Chairman of The Ark, a unique cultural center for children in Dublin.

DECLAN QUINN (Director of Photography)

Declan Quinn, the son of Irish immigrants to America himself, brings his unique creative touch to *In America*. Quinn is perhaps best known for creating the muted, yet penetrating look of the Academy Award-winning *Leaving Las Vegas*, which won him the IFP Award for Best Cinematography. His recent work includes Mira Nair's *Monsoon Wedding* and her HBO film *Hysterical Blindness*, as well as her forthcoming *Vanity Fair* starring

Reese Witherspoon. Quinn also recently reunited with Mike Figgis to shoot the thriller *Cold Creek Manor* with Dennis Quaid and Sharon Stone.

Quinn's many feature credits include Joel Schumacher's *Flawless*; Betty Thomas' *28 Days*, *One True Thing*; the indie film *2X4* (for which he won the 1998 Sundance Film Festival Best Cinematography Award); Mira Nair's *Kama Sutra*, which won him a second IFP Award for Best Cinematography; and *This Is My Father*, which starred his brother Aidan Quinn and was directed by his other brother, Paul Quinn.

Other credits include Mike Figgis' *One Night Stand; Vanya on 42nd Street*, with director Louis Malle; and *All Things Bright and Beautiful* for director Barry Devlin, among others. Quinn's TV credits include *Fallen Angels* for which he was nominated for a CableAce Award for Best Cinematography. His documentary credits include rehearsal and tour films for R.E.M., the U2 tour films *Outside America* and *The Unforgettable Fire*, and *Cousin Bobby*.

MARK GERAGHTY (Production Designer)

Mark Geraghty most recently designed *The Count of Monte Cristo* for director Kevin Reynolds. He has worked as a production designer on an extensive list of high quality films and TV dramas including *Rat, When the Sky Falls, Dancing at Lughnasa, Welcome to Sarajevo, The Run of the Country, Nothing Personal, An Awfully Big Adventure,* and *The Young Indiana Jones Chronicles*. He has has collaborated on three of Roddy Doyle's contemporary Dublin stories, Stephen Frears's *The Van* and *The Snapper* and Michael Winterbottom's TV drama series *Family*. He has worked as an art director on Mike Newell's *Into the West*, Alan Parker's acclaimed urban musical *The Commitments*, Don Bluth's animation feature *Rock-a-Doodle* and Jim Sheridan's Oscar-winning *My Left Foot*.

CAST

SAMANTHA MORTON (Sarah)

Samantha Morton won a London Film Critics Award and earned Academy Award and Golden Globe nominations in 2000 for her role opposite Sean Penn in Woody Allen's *Sweet and Lowdown*. Recently she was seen opposite Tom Cruise in Steven Spielberg's sci-fi epic *Minority Report*, for which she won a Best Actress Empire Award; in Alison McLean's *Jesus' Son* based on the book by Denis Johnson; and in Lynne Ramsay's *Morvern Callar* for which she won a Best Actress British Independent Film Award and was nominated for Best Actress by the London Film Critics. Morton will next be seen with Tim Robbins in Michael Winterbottom's *Code 46.*

Morton's feature film debut in Carine Adler's *Under the Skin* received widespread critical attention, garnering her a Best Actress Award from The Boston Society of Film Critics, and a nomination for Best Actress at the British Independent Film Awards in 1998. Her additional credits include Julien Temple's *Pandaemonium*; Amos Gitae's *Eden*; *This Is the Sea*, with Gabriel Byrne; *Dreaming of Joseph Lees*, for which she won the Evening Standard's Best Actress Award; and *The Last Yellow*, directed by Julian Farino. She has been seen in the television films "Band of Gold," "Cracker," "Jane Eyre" (as Jane Eyre), "Tom Jones" and the mini-series "Emma," based on Jane Austen's novel.

PADDY CONSIDINE (Johnny)

Paddy Considine was most recently seen in Michael Winterbottom's critically acclaimed story of the Manchester music scene, *24 Hour Party People*. He first came to the fore as the obsessive loner in the British indie *A Room for Romeo Brass*, directed by Shane Meadows, and drew further accolades for his work as the love-sick Alfie in Pawel Pawlikowski's award-winning *The Last Resort*. He has just finished shooting Pawlikowski's *My Summer of Love*.

Considine's other films include *Happy Now, The Martins,* and the short film *My Wrongs #8245-8249 & 117,* which won the BAFTA Award. Considine's upcoming films include Shane Meadows' untitled project, which is co-written by Considine.

DJIMON HOUNSOU (Mateo)

Djimon Hounsou received a Golden Globe nomination for his performance as Cinque, the rebel slave leader in *Amistad*. He went on to star in the Academy Award-winning epic *Gladiator*, in which he played Juba, the fiery warrior who befriends Maximus (Russell Crowe). His recent work includes Shekhar Kapur's *The Four Feathers, Biker Boyz* with Laurence Fishburne, *Lara Croft Tomb Raider: The Cradle of Life* directed by Jan De Bont, and the forthcoming *Muraya* from director Jan Kounen.

Born in Benin, West Africa, Hounsou moved to Paris at the age of thirteen for his education. At twenty-two, he was discovered by fashion designer Thierry Mugler, who immediately featured him in several of his design campaigns, as well as in his book *Thierry Mugler Photographs*. Hounsou was also a subject in the late Herb Ritts' book *Men and Women*. Hounsou was subsequently spotted by director David Fincher (*Fight Club, Seven*), who cast him in three music videos: Steve Winwood's "Roll With It," Madonna's "Express Yourself" and Paula Abdul's "Straight Up." Once established as an international model, Hounsou made the move to Los Angeles where he taught himself English (largely by watching television documentaries) and broke into acting. A featured role in the Janet Jackson video "Love Will Never Do Without You" caught the attention of agents and casting directors and led to roles in such films as *Stargate, Unlawful Entry,* and *Deep Rising*, before landing the career-making role in Steven Spielberg's *Amistad*. Hounsou has also been seen in a recurring role on television's popular *E.R.*

SARAH BOLGER (Christy)

In America marks eleven-year-old Sarah Bolger's second feature film. Her first was *A Love Divided* for director Sydney Macartney. For television, Bolger appeared in "A Secret Affair." Her voice will soon be heard on a new cartoon entitled "The World of Tosh." Bolger will next be seen in the smtv/BBC Television's "The Yo Yo."

She and her sister, Emma, who plays her sister in the film, reside in Ireland and study drama with the Young Peoples Theatre/Ann Kavanagh School.

EMMA BOLGER (Ariel)

In America marks seven-year-old Emma Bolger's acting debut. She and her sister, Sarah, who plays her sister in the film, reside in Ireland and study drama with the Young Peoples Theatre/Ann Kavanagh School.

cast and crew credits

FOX SEARCHLIGHT PICTURES Presents
A HELL'S KITCHEN Production

IN AMERICA

SAMANTHA MORTON   PADDY CONSIDINE   DJIMON HOUNSOU

Music Composed by
**GAVIN FRIDAY and
MAURICE SEEZER**

Costume Designer
EIMER NI MHAOLDOMHNAIGH

Edited by
NAOMI GERAGHTY

Production Designer
MARK GERAGHTY

Director of Photography
DECLAN QUINN

Co-Producer
PAUL MYLER

Produced by
**JIM SHERIDAN
ARTHUR LAPPIN**

Written by
**JIM SHERIDAN &
NAOMI SHERIDAN &
KIRSTEN SHERIDAN**

Directed by
JIM SHERIDAN

"AN ANGLO-IRISH CO-PRODUCTION"
www.foxsearchlight.com

CAST IN ORDER OF APPEARANCE

johnny	paddy considine
sarah	samantha morton
christy	sarah bolger
ariel	emma bolger
immigration officer #1	neal jones
immigration officer # 2	randall carlton
frankie	ciaran cronin
mateo	djimon hounsou
papo	juan hernandez
blind man	nye heron
tony	jason salkey
steve	rene millan
papo's girlfriend	sara james
theatre director	bob gallico
assistant theatre director	jason killalee
mexican woman with child	chary o'dea
shopkeeper	adrian martinez
marina	merrina millsapp
barker	david wike
man at fair	guy carleton
nun on school steps	elaine grollman
gynaecologist	nick dunning
frank	michael sean tighe
angela	jennifer seifert
prize giving nun	kathleen king
nun playing piano	eilish scanlon
actor in queue	tom murphy
stockbrocker in taxi	des bishop
hospital administrator	bernadette quigley
paediatrician	frank wood
sarah mateo	molly glynn
thomas bakewell	jer o'leary
administrator / nurse	regina roe
hospital receptionist	tamla clarke
doctor	carmen regan
hospice nurse	nisha nayar

mexican man guitarist	**rodrigo pineda sanchez**
mexican woman guitarist lopez	**gabriela quintero**
stunt coordinator	**manny siverio**
johnny stunt double	**norman douglass**
stunts	**jeff ward**
	danny aiello III
	cort hessler III
	don hewitt
dog	**bootsu**

CREW

production manager	*jo homewood*
1st assistant director	*konrad jay*
2nd assistant director	*karen richards*
associate producer	*nye heron*
post production supervisor	*maria walker*
third assistant director	*raymond kirk*
crowd coordinators	*jillian wilson*
	jill dempsey
trainee assistant director	*susan stanley*
steadicam operator	*vince mcgahon*
steadicam operator & 2nd unit director of photography	
	howard smith
additional photography	*martin little*
	naomi sheridan
focus puller	*ciaran kavanagh*
clapper loader	*owen farrell*
camera trainee	*andrew o'reilly*
video assist / *operator*	*gareth nevin*
grip	*john murphy*
stills photographer	*bernard walsh*
sound mixer /	
production sound recordist	*daniel birch*
boom operator	*richard hetherington*
sound trainee	*andrew felton*
first assistant editor	*mairead mcivor*

avid assistant editor	*nicky dunne*
second assistant editor	*linda nartey*
trainee editors	*siobhan mcmahon,*
	james watt
conforming assistant	*lalit goyal*
locations manager	*paddy mccarney*
assistant locations managers	*naoise barry*
	edmund sampson
locations trainee / assistant	
	erinn thompson
art director	*susie cullen*
construction manager	*russ bailey*
set decorator	*johnny byrne*
production buyer	*jenny oman*
assistant art director	*ciara gormley*
draughtsman	*conor devlin*
art department trainee	*aeveen fleming*
storyboard artist	*bruce ryder*
property master	*eamonn o'higgins*
chargehand dressing prop	*alan dunne*
dressing props	*eoin lewis, david wallace*
stand-by props	*nuala mckernan,*
	daragh lewis
trainee props	*tyrone monaghan,*
aran byrne	
prop runaround driver	*breffni winston*
script supervisor	*louise gaffney*
assistant costume designer	
	judith williams
wardrobe supervisor	*judith devlin*
wardrobe assistant	*sharon beatty*
wardrobe trainees	*leonie prendergast*
	debbie millington
chief hairdresser	*orla carroll*
assistant hairdresser	*una o'sullivan*
key make-up artist	*morna ferguson*
assistant make-up artist	*niamh o'loan*

stand-by carpenter	david oldham
stand-by painter	darren kearney
stand-by rigger	robert reilly
stand-by stagehand	jimmy gillen
supervising carpenter	paul keogh
carpenters	eugene campbell, matthew kirwan, ken carlisle, stephen driver
master painter	robbie richardson
painters	gary o'donnell, gerard richardson, lar griffin, daniel lyons
stagehands	timmy crimmins, shane donnelly, tony kelly
riggers	paul tracey, steve montague, james merrigan, eamon kelly
chargehand carpenter	john greene
apprentice carpenter	michael o'toole
construction runaround	ian wallace
gaffer	james maguire
best boy	eoin o'hagan
electricians	niall mannion, noel holland
practical electricians	john carr, dermot coleman
generator operator	stephen mccarthy
production coordinator	carol moorhead
assistant coordinator	maire doherty
production secretary	ingrid goodwin
producers' assistant	una spillane
production assistant	grainne macanthony
assistant to ms. morton	tara slye
production executive, hell's kitchen	niamh nolan
accountant, hell's kitchen	sue henderson
production executive, hell's kitchen, los angeles	renata adamidov
assistant to jim sheridan	joanne kelly
production consultant	simon carmody
production accountant	rory mac dermott
assistant accountant	clare cunningham
accounts assistant	billie webster
accounts trainee	mel gallagher
transport captain / transport coordinator	jimmy cullen
unit drivers	ernie beakhurst, geoff cullen, tony cullen, derek pomeroy, jimmy devlin
drivers	eddie cullen, noel burke, dracey jobbins, willie cooley, john keelihan, tony clarke, john kavanagh, jason cullen, gerry malone, philip murphy
action vehicle coordinator	stephen carroll
special effects	team fx
special effects coordinators	brendan byrne, pat redmond
special effects crew	aidan byrne, dermot byrne, martin fitzpatrick, kevin kearns
stunt coordinator	joe condren
unit nurse	eileen conroy
utility stand-ins	enda doherty, adrienne greenhalgh, nessa linnane
unit publicist	gerry lundberg publicity
catering	hot buns catering
chaperone	monica bolger
tutor	lucie nunan
nutritionist	julie dowsett
animal handler	copsewood aviaries
voice coach	gerry grennell
dialect coach	brooks baldwin
mateo's paintings and signage	laurence o'toole
scenic artists	steve mitchell, dave packard
medical consultant	carmel regan

NEW YORK UNIT

line producer NY unit	meredith zamsky
production supervisor	patricia adlesic
first assistant director	michael lerman
production accountant	beth zagrany
second assistant director	carrie fix
second second assistant director	alyson latz
key set production assistant	joe smalley
set production assistants	mariela comitini, tracy ershow, david gross, kristin hensley, christopher sanata
additional production assistants	henry saan, hope walter, frank slaten
'A' camera / steadicam operator	william arnot
first assistant camera	robert mancuso
second assistant camera	amanda hudson
film loader / clapper loader	hollis meminge
first assistant camera – 'B' camera	a. chris silano
director of photography	gerard sava
stills photographer	barry wetcher
sound mixer / stand by	ken ishii
boom operator	paul koronkiewicz
boom / cable	kim maitland
assistant editor	james e. (eddie) nichols, jr.
location manager	georg schmithusen
assistant location manager	wende kremer
location assistants	frank cattano, jose guerrero
location scout – baltimore	william (b.j.) spencer
parking coordinator	maurice cabrera
art director	wing lee
assistant art director	stephen carter
art department coordinator	alex wei
prop master	william f. reynolds
assistant prop masters	ruth dipasquale, steve scanlon
gaffer	robert sciretta
best boy	robert mcgavin
electricians	john mitchell, fred johanns, ozzie phothivongsa
assistant costume designer	joan kauffman
wardrobe supervisors	catherine george, mark burchard
chief hairdresser	angel deangelis haiko
key make-up artist	lori hicks
production coordinators	sandra saccio, kerin ferallo
office production assistant	marc santo
additional production assistants	edward (teddy) yoon, peter harrison
payroll accountant	patricia porter
accounting assistant	james lovaglio
construction coordinator	ken hammer
construction foreman	k. scott gertsen
key construction grip	david mcallister
carpenter	robert keller

rigging gaffer	thomas ford
shop electrician	paul steinberg
transport captain / teamster captain	james whalen
drivers	michael canosa, michael connolly, brendan connolly, joseph buonocore, jr., joe feathersone, steve szucs, steven curtis, tom horvath, wesley petersen, paul kane, mike buchman, frank appecilli, george o'neill, kris keefe, ted brown
special effects supervisor	steven kirshoff
background casting	grant wilfley casting
catering	shooting stars catering
chef	brian brown
1st assistant chef	winston stewart
2nd assistant chef	lisa brown
craft service	nelson puente
charge scenic	warren jorgenson
scenic	alex gorodetsky
set decorator	kate kennedy
leadman	philip c. canfield
set dressers	scott canfield, christopher heaps, patrice longo
on set dressers	anthony baldasare
storyboard artist	john f. davis
tutor	joan b. benjamin, on location education
video playback	douglas a. martines
key grip	james finnerty, jr.
best boy grip	john p. dolan
dolly grip	joe donohue
grips	christopher purificato, john finnerty, joseph finnerty

NEW YORK SNOW UNIT

coordinator	don kelly
digital cameraman	michael canzoniero
super 16 cameraman	john inwood
mini dv cameraman	matt loguercio
digital cameraman	marco ricci

ADDITIONAL PHOTOGRAPHY

second assistant director	therese friel
third assistant director	alexandra jones
crowd coordinator	georgina short
trainee assistant director	jenny maloney
focus puller	eamon o'keefe
clapper loader	fionn comerford
grip	joe quigley
sound trainee	brian connolly
locations manager	dougal cousins
assistant locations manager	niall martin
locations trainee	ciaran pattan
supervising art director	fiona daly
art director	vivienne gray
construction coordinator	tom dowling
assistant art director	nicola moroney
production buyer	sarah kingston
property master	dave peters
stand-by props	joshua barraud
script supervisor	jeanette mcgrath
wardrobe assistant	clodagh deegan
wardrobe trainee	michelle butler
stand-by carpenter	mark cannon
stand-by painter	thomas o'shaughnessy
stand-by rigger	tom tormey

stand-by stagehand	*john delaney*
electricians	*louis conroy,*
	david durney,
	graeme haughton, maurice swan
assistant accountant	*emer egan*
construction supervisor	*darren crimmins*
carpenters	*eugene campbell, gay cotes,*
	david byrne, paul kearney,
	gavin flanagan, stephen broughal
master painter	*christy o'shaughnessy*
painters	*bronwyn r clohissey*
	philip o'shaughnessy
supervising plasterer	*jimmy irwin*
stagehand	*mick mulvanney*
rigger	*william o'brien*
unit drivers	*alan barton,*
	john mcguinness
prop runaround driver	*niall o'h-uadhaigh*
camera car driver	*patrick gillligan*
construction runaround	*maurice thompson*
unit nurse	*theresa gantley*
catering	*teamwork catering*
utility stand-ins	*alan warter*
	zeke lawless

POST PRODUCTION

supervising sound editor	*nigel mills*
dialogue/adr editor	*philip alton*
additional dialogue editor	*richard fettes*
effects editor	*lewis goldstein*
foley editor	*mike wood*
music editor	*michael connell*
assistant sound editor	*steve mayer*
assistant dialogue editor	*conor mackey*
assistant adr editor	*michael lemass*
foley artists	*paula boran, ruth sullivan*
adr mixers	*david boulton,*
	john bateman,
	peter gleaves
adr recordists	*brian gallagher,*
	colette dahanne
re-recording mixers	*timothy cavagin,*
	teve single
recordist	*don bell*
recordist's assistant	*peter isaac*
sound maintenance	*graham nieder*
dolby engineer	*alex hudd*
sound post production	
	twickenham film studios
original music written arranged &	
produced by	*gavin friday &*
	maurice seezer:
	© *blue mountain music 2002*
performed by	
	"the friday/seezer ensemble"
	maurice seezer – piano, keyboards,
	organ, accordion
	renaud pion – woodwinds
	michael blair – drums, percussion,
	tuned percussioon
	des moore – guitars, banjo, mandolin
	gareth hughes – bass,
	miriam roycroft – cello
with	*stephen mc donnell – trumpet*
	triona marshall – harp
the irish film orchestra	
conducted by	*brian byrne*
orchestrations by	*maurice seezer*
orchestra managment	*catriona walsh*

recorded at	*windmill lane studios.*
	dublin
all music recorded and mixed by	*andrew*
	boland
assistant engineer	*kieran lynch*
assistant	*mark dwyer*
studio manager	*catherine rutter*
music pre-production	*"the horse studio"*
	dublin
friday / seezer legal & business affairs	
	gaby smyth
legal consultant	*barbara galavan*
friday / seezer security	*muttley*
special thanks to	*maria pizzuti*
music supervisor	*david donohue*

FACILITIES AND SUPPLIERS

title design	*frameline*
visual effects by	*mill film, shepperton*
visual effects supervisor	
	simon stanley-clamp
visual effects producer	*susi roper*
sequence supervisor	*dan pettipher*
digital compositors	*mark bakowski,*
	helen ball, richard little, simon carr
visual effects coordinator	*andrew jeffery*
negative cutting	*p.n.c.*
film laboratory	*technicolor ltd, uk*
film lab coordinator	*keith bryant*
grader	*peter hunt*
film stock	*kodak uk ltd / photologic*
post production facility	
	windmill lane studios, dublin
avid supplied by	*london editing machines*
lighting	*cine electric*
travel agent	*flair travel*
accountants	*kpmg*
payroll services	*sargent-disc ltd.*
bankers	*bank of ireland*
legal advisors	*olswang*
	matheson ormsby prentice
insurance	*risk management*
	aon insurance
completion bond	*cinefinance*
security	*oisin security*
sound equipment supplied by	
	daniel birch sound equipment
accommodation	
	access conference connections
facilities provided by	*e.c. transport*
walkie talkies supplied by	*theatrical arms*
couriers	*aerfast*
adr	*ardmore sound, sound one,*
	new york

SONGS

"Ezee Does It"
Written by Beast /
Michael Dwaine Wallace
Published by Extreme Music Library plc
Courtesy of Extreme Music Library plc

"Aranci Daterri!"
From La Boheme by Giacomo Puccini
Performed by La Scala Opera Chorus and
Orchestra, Milan
Conducted by Umberto Berretoni
Licensed courtesy of HNH International Ltd.

"Cherry Coke & Pizza Pie"
Performed by The Mutts
Written by Hakan Akesson
Courtesy of LoveCat Records
Published by Big Tiger Music (BMI)
By arrangement with Ocean Park Music Group

"Arrow From My Heart"
Written by Evan Olson
Performed by Bus Stop
Courtesy of LoveCat Records
Published by Big Tiger Music (BMI)
By arrangement with Ocean Park Music Group

"Der Fischer"
Performed by Aylish E. Kerrigan,
Mezzosoprano
Accompanied by Andreas Kersten, piano
Composed by Franz Schubert
Text by J.W.V. Goethe

"Quando M'en Vo'soletta"
From La Boheme by Giacomo Puccini
Performed by La Scala Opera Chorus and
Orchestra, Milan
Soprano Tatiana Menotti
Conducted by Umberto Berretoni
Licensed courtesy of HNH
International Ltd.

"Do You Believe in Magic"
Performed by The Lovin' Spoonful
Written by John Sebastian
Published by Robbins Music Corporation Ltd. /
EMI Music Publishing Ltd.
Licenced courtesy of Buddah Records / BMG
U.K. & Ireland Ltd.

"Baby I'm Real"
Performed by Kid Creole and The Coconuts
Written by August Darnell
Published by Ascot Music for the World, Love-
Cat Music and Jessica & Jonathan Music for
USA & Canada
Courtesy of Atoll Music and
LoveCat Music
By arrangement with Ocean Park
Music Group

"Beach Bomb"
Written by Kent Buchanon
Published by Extreme Music Library plc
Courtesy of Extreme Music Library plc

"La Cubanita"
Performed by Los Ninos De Sara
Written by Antoine Santiago, Jean Motos, Ramon
Campos & Antoine Contreras
Published by Ascot Music for the World, LoveCat
Music and Jessica & Jonathan Music for USA &
Canada
Courtesy of Atoll Music and LoveCat Music
By arrangement with Ocean Park Music Group

"La Bamba"
Trad. Arr. by El Son
Published by Extreme Music Library plc
Courtesy of Extreme Music Library plc

"Stuck Together"
Written by Freddie Funk
Published by Extreme Music Library plc
Courtesy of Extreme Music Library plc

Illustrated with more than 70 full-color photographs, this charming book captures writer/director/ producer Jim Sheridan's most personal and magical story yet, the tale of a family finding its soul, *In America*, which he co-wrote with his daughters, Naomi Sheridan and Kirsten Sheridan. Based on his own experiences coming to New York as a flat-broke immigrant, as well as remembrances of a devastating family tragedy, *In America* confronts the mysterious nature of love, loss, and finding new hope.

With forewords by the screenwriters detailing their writing process and revealing unbelievable moments from their own journey to America in the 1980s, this lovely portrait of the film includes the entire screenplay, an illuminating conversation between Jim Sheridan and Columbia University's Director of Undergraduate Film Studies Annette Insdorf, biographies of the filmmakers and actors, and the full cast and crew credits.

$22

A NEWMARKET PICTORIAL MOVIEBOOK
NEWMARKET PRESS • NEW YORK
www.newmarketpress.com
Cover design by Deborah Daly.

ISBN 1-55704-61
52
9 781557 046185